THE DUCATI BIBLE

860, 900 & Mille
All models 1975 to 1986

DESMO

900 **SUPER SPORT**

DUCATI

VELOCE PUBLISHING
THE PUBLISHER OF FINE AUTOMOTIVE BOOKS

CONTENTS

INTRODUCTION

When it was conceived in 1973, Ducati's bevel-drive square-case engine was envisaged as a more modern replacement for the round-case 750. Although only in production for two years, the 750 engine was already seen as too labour intensive to manufacture, and would have difficulty meeting future noise and left-side gearshift legislation. With the 750 barely in production Ducati's great engineer Ing. Fabio Taglioni set to work updating the bevel-drive twin, differentiating it with angular, polished aluminium outer engine cases and a capacity of 864cc. This engine would have a lifespan considerably longer than that of the round-case 750, and ultimately power a wider range of motorcycles.

That the 750 engine would evolve into an 860 was probably inevitable. The precedence for capacity increases was set with the overhead camshaft single that grew from 350 to 436cc in 1969. Taglioni also told a press conference in London in January 1971 that the 750 twin would be an 860 for the US when it went into production. This didn't eventuate, however, and the first official 860 was the 1973 Barcelona endurance racer. The racer was based on the round-case, and the production 860 that appeared during 1974 was considerably redesigned. Not only did the engine look quite different, it incorporated a stronger bevel-gear camshaft drive, electronic ignition, an oil filter, and a left-side gearshift. The new engine promised lower production costs, increased reliability, and no loss of performance with quieter mufflers.

Initially, the 864cc engine was intended only for the Giugiaro-designed 860 GT, and Taglioni designed square engine covers to match this angular body shape. But the failure of the 860 GT saw the resurrection of the Super Sport, the angular engine covers successfully complementing the rounder style Super Sport bodywork. The 860 became a 900 (without any actual capacity increase), and several design updates were incorporated over the years, while the distinctive square outer engine covers were retained. It wasn't until 1983 that these covers were redesigned, this time for the final series of 900 and the Mille. In all incarnations, 860, 900, Mille, valve spring or desmo, the square-case engine was one of Ducati's most significant, and the motorcycles it powered were some of the most iconic. They were fantastic motorcycles that deserve their strong following.

Researching a book that covers so many variations on a theme is difficult. Factory records recording engine and frame numbers no longer exist, and my own database of over 3500 machines has been a primary source of information. Every attempt has been made to provide the correct information regarding the specification of individual models, but there will always be some inconsistency. The era of the early 1980s was particularly difficult to categorise as Ducati Meccanica was struggling to remain profitable and worker morale was low. As motorcycle production gradually diminished, so did some uniformity.

My own experience with these motorcycles spans more than thirty years. After seeing a new 900 Super Sport at the 1975 Earls Court

Motorcycle Show, a long-term yearning led to eventual ownership. Before that, I bought a new 900 SD Darmah, 900 and Mille Mike Hailwood Replicas, and restored several Darmahs and Super Sports. When it came to writing this book I was fortunate to have access to all factory technical bulletins of the period and all spare parts lists, workshop and owners' manuals accumulated over the years. When selecting photos I have endeavoured to use as many period photographs as possible. This was only possible through the generosity of magazine editors, particularly Jeremy Bowdler of *Two Wheels* magazine, and David Edwards of *Cycle World* magazine. Livio Lodi of Museo Ducati provided many factory publicity pictures as well as full production data. Those who provided photos, or perfectly original machines for photography, were Philip Ayres, Nico Georgeoglou, Tony Hannagan, Rob van Klootwijk, and Tim O'Mahony. The Bevelheads internet forum was particularly helpful, with many enthusiasts providing details of their 900 Ducatis. Thanks go to the following:

Richard Albee
Steve Allen
Joseph Ballardini
Ian Brunton
Charlie Clancy
Brad Claypool

Gonzalo Costas
Rick Covello
Steve Craven
Denis De Jong
Dean Deeds
Roger Donnan
Seth Dorfler
Tim Doucette
Ian Ellison
Kjell Eriksson
Roy Fincham
Peter Freiberger
Craig Hunley
Mark Kaczmarczyk
Tim Keyes
Rob Labordus
Rich Lambrechts
Robbie Marais
Bob Marren
Bob McKeehan

Brent Meldrum
David Messenger
Dennis Milani
Tim Moores
Paul O'Grady
Gerard Oosterwijk
Colin Parker
Geoff Priest
Tod Rafferty
Gene Rankin
Ken Reece
Glenn Scanlon
Paul Skippen
Mark Trayford
Juhani Virtanen
Noel Watson
Knut Wille
Roderick Withnell
Rick Yamane

As always, thanks go to my family, my wife Miriam and sons Ben and Tim, who continue to enthusiastically endorse my work. I would also like to thank Rod Grainger and the team at Veloce for their support with this project.

Ian Falloon

CHAPTER ONE

PRELUDE

The great engineer Fabio Taglioni was responsible for all the important Ducati designs until the mid-1980s. This photo was taken in his home in 1998, with a wooden mock-up of his proposed 1000cc V-four in the background.

The release of the 860 GT in 1974 signalled a change in direction for Ducati. Although for many enthusiasts the end of the classic 750 round-case and overhead camshaft singles represented a death knell, the reality was far different. The 860 did not immediately earn the following of the earlier 750, but historically it became considerably more significant. Whereas 750 production lasted just four years (and only 6159 examples), the 860 square-case (and subsequent Mille) was built for 12 years. There were many more varieties, and total production was substantially more at 27,483 motorcycles. Although the 750 round-case has been the main focus for those interested in historical Ducatis, the square-case 860 was really the archetypal Ducati of the 1970s.

To understand why the 860 was created we need to go back to the end of the 1960s. Following a series of dubious commercial ventures, including the distribution of British Triumph cars in Italy, Ducati was in a precarious financial position. Requiring immediate capital, Ducati Meccanica was placed under direct government control as part of the EFIM (Ente Finanziaria per gli Industrie Metalmeccaniche) group at the end of 1969. New directors (Arnaldo Milvio, Fredmano Spairani, and Cosimo Calcagnile) were appointed and were instrumental in changing the direction of the company. During 1970, Ducati's great engineer Ing. Fabio Taglioni was encouraged to develop the new 750 twin and 500 Grand Prix racer. Milvio stated in a press release late in 1970 that he wanted a 750cc roadster, because big machines were the trend, and to get back into racing to publicise the Ducati name and prove its products. In a further press conference at the London Olympia Show in January 1971 Milvio stated that an 860cc version of the 750 would be produced for the US market. Already the seeds were sown for the 860.

There was no doubt that the release of the round-case 750 rejuvenated the company, but implementation of the production 750 was delayed due to the late construction of the new 36,000 square metre building adjacent to the existing factory. Completion of this building took longer than anticipated, and wasn't operational until the end of 1972. In the meantime, Ducati won the Imola 200 Formula 750 race and was riding a wave of success it hadn't previously experienced. Demand for the 750 was strong all around the world but Ducati simply didn't have the facilities to build it in large numbers. Ducati also found it near impossible to mass produce the 750 engine as it was so complex and time consuming to assemble. With its abundance of shims and interdependent gears each engine took one worker six hours to assemble from scratch, and this was uneconomic. While the Ducati 750 was on everyone's lips as the world-beating 750, only 519 twins were produced during 1972. There was simply no way the company could sustain its expensive racing program with such low production numbers, and the directors were held accountable.

As he had been with Ducati since 1956 and understood the commercial operation Calcagnile was spared, but Milvio and Spairani paid for their extravagance. Spairani departed to MV Agusta at the end of 1972, and Milvio was moved to another company within the EFIM Group (Isotta Fraschini) early in 1973. He was replaced by Ing. Cristiano de Eccher (previously with Aermacchi prior to its sale to AMF in America) who immediately implemented cost cutting and increased production.

De Eccher instructed Taglioni to begin the redesign of the expensive 750cc bevel-drive engine so it was cheaper to manufacture, and he cut the racing program. The 1973 racing program was to include only two events; the Imola 200 and the Bol d'Or 24-hour race, and factory development of the 500 Grand Prix racer was suspended. Taglioni managed to persuade de Eccher to sanction an entry in the Barcelona 24-hour race as well as the Bol d'Or but the halcyon days of racing were over for the time being.

In October 1973, Ing. de Eccher announced at a press conference that Ducati would produce 15,000 motorcycles in 1974. Citing excessive production costs and difficulties in meeting increasing noise and emissions legislation, de Eccher indicated that the 750 would be replaced by the 860 GT. At the same time the overhead camshaft singles would make way for a new parallel twin. Besides being cheaper to manufacture, quieter, and more environmentally friendly, the 860 GT would also meet forthcoming left-side gearshift requirements in the US.

Unlike earlier managers (Montano, Milvio and Spairani) de Eccher wasn't a motorcycle enthusiast. He wasn't particularly interested in the emotional or aesthetic aspect of motorcycles, only sales, and engaged automobile designer Giorgetto Giugiaro to style the 860. Giugiaro came with some impressive automotive credentials but he had little motorcycle experience, and Giugiaro and Ducati's engineers spent most of 1973 on the 860 project. As the engine for the 860 was also considerably redesigned, it took longer than expected for production to be implemented. The 860 GT finally went into production in September 1974, after the summer break, and was available early in 1975 alongside stocks of unsold 750s.

The 860 Prototype

Considering Ducati had a history of building similar engines in multiple displacements, it was no surprise to see the 750 grow to an 860 during 1973. The wide-crankcase, overhead camshaft single

first introduced at the end of 1967 as a 350 became a 450 in 1969. At around the same time, Taglioni prepared a racing 450cc desmodromic single for Bruno Spaggiari and, by 1973, had considerable experience with 86mm racing pistons. The 1973 Imola 750 racers featured 86mm pistons and, for the 1973 Barcelona 24-Hour endurance race in July, Taglioni built a machine based on the production 750 Sport. 864cc was achieved by combining the 86mm cylinders with the production 750 74.4mm stroke. From the 1973 Imola racer came a dry clutch, 60-degree desmodromic cylinder heads, 40mm Dell'Orto carburettors, and a high-rise exhaust system. The 180kg 860 was eminently suited to the tight and twisting 3.62km Montjuich Park circuit, especially in the hands of local experts Salvador Canellas and 1972 race winner Benjamin Grau. They won in record time, covering 1674.58 miles at 71mph. In September the same machine was entered for the Bol d'Or at Le Mans, but Canellas and Grau retired before half distance. The victory in the 1973 Barcelona race was one of Ducatis's greatest victories and, while the 860 racer was basically a factory round-case 750, it provided the 860 displacement a significance that would be sustained for the rest of the decade and beyond.

There was another, more pragmatic, reason for the creation of the 860. Even by 1973 there was no doubt that legislation was beginning to catch up with the 750 GT. Noise restrictions would soon mean an end to the distinctive Conti exhaust system with its loud bark, and bikes manufactured after September 1974 would need to shift on the left-side to be able to be sold in the United States. The only way that the already modest performance of the 750 GT could be maintained with further inlet and exhaust restrictions was by enlarging the engine.

At around the same time as Taglioni was preparing the first 860cc racer, a 750 GT was despatched to Giorgetto Giugiaro's ItalDesign Studio at Moncalieri in Turin. Giugiaro was born on 7 August 1938 in Garessio, near Cuneo in the Piedmont region, and began his career with Fiat at the age of 17 years. Towards the end of 1959 he joined Bertone, where he designed the Alfa Romeo Giulia GT and Fiat 850 Spider. Giugiaro moved to head Ghia's design studio at the end of 1965 where he was responsible for several landmark designs, notably the Maserati Ghibli and De Tomaso Pampero. In 1967 Giugiaro established ItalDesign and, in the early 1970s, initiated the 'folded paper' looks of straight lines and hard edges. The first example of this style was the Lotus Esprit of 1972, followed by the

Volkswagen Golf, Hyundai Pony and the Lancia Delta. In was within this design climate that the 860 was created. Although it seemed incongruous to commission an automotive design studio to style the 860, Giugiaro was already expanding his design parameters beyond cars and, after the 860, moved into cameras, telephones and electrical appliances.

Fabio Taglioni, in an interview with the author in 1995, said it was Cristiano de Eccher who commissioned Giugiaro to design the 860. Prior to the 860 most Ducati styling was done in-house, or by Leopoldo Tartarini who was closely associated with the factory. De Eccher allowed Giugiaro total control of the eventual product and Taglioni recalled Giugiaro requesting the engine cases be redesigned to comply with his 'folded paper' vision.

As the prototype 860 needed to be ready for the Milan Show in November 1973, it remained essentially a cosmetically-modified 750. The earliest mock-up retained the 750 GT leading axle front fork, 19in front wheel, and wide rear

subframe bent upwards at the rear. For the Milan Show prototype the front wheel was changed to an 18in Borrani, and the fork was a Ceriani centre-axle with a single Brembo disc brake. The frame was considerably modified at the rear, but at this stage retained the 750-style straight front downtubes. The rear subframe was narrowed with the rear shock absorber mounts outside the frame tubes, and this prototype already had the swingarm with eccentric adjusters for chain adjustment that featured on the 1973 Imola 750 factory racers. The yellow and black bodywork included angular mudguards, fuel tank, seat and side covers, a small headlight nacelle fairing, and faired taillight assembly. The ignition switch was located under the fuel tank on the left, and there were new style CEV handlebar switches. The later distinctive Giugiaro graphics had yet to appear.

By the time of the Milan Show Taglioni had also managed to redesign the engine, internally and externally. The prototype included an electric start, and many of the features of the eventual production version (oil filter, revised camshaft

drive, and electronic ignition). This prototype retained the right-side gearshift and left-side brake, and included larger and quieter Lafranconi mufflers. When displayed at Milan the 860 didn't exactly cause a sensation as it was overshadowed by the new 750 Super Sport desmodromic 'Imola' replica. Milan 1973 was really the show for the sporting 750 with Laverda showing its new 750 SFC and Moto Guzzi the 750 S.

While its appearance at Milan was greeted with only mild enthusiasm, Ing. De Eccher had already made it clear the 860 was to replace the 750 during 1974. Test rider Raoul Martini continued its development and, by March 1974, the small headlight fairing had disappeared. The taillight was changed to a larger type similar to that fitted to the US specification 750 GT, and angular turn signals were installed. At this stage the gearshift

A publicity photo of the late-1973 860 prototype, now with square engine cases and an electric start. (Courtesy Ducati Motor)

was still on the right, but a left-side conversion was soon tested. A few months later another prototype appeared, painted black and white. This now had a left-side gearshift but retained the Borrani alloy wheel rims and featured in some advertising material. Difficulties continued during 1974. The factory was beset by rolling strikes and there were many problems with the supply of proprietary components from outside suppliers. Ducati couldn't meet its production target ,and only 7703 motorcycles were produced in 1974. The company could only hope the situation would improve for 1975, and the 860 would be its saviour.

Factory drawings for the 860cc square-case engine, with both valve spring and desmodromic cylinder heads. (Courtesy Ducati Motor)

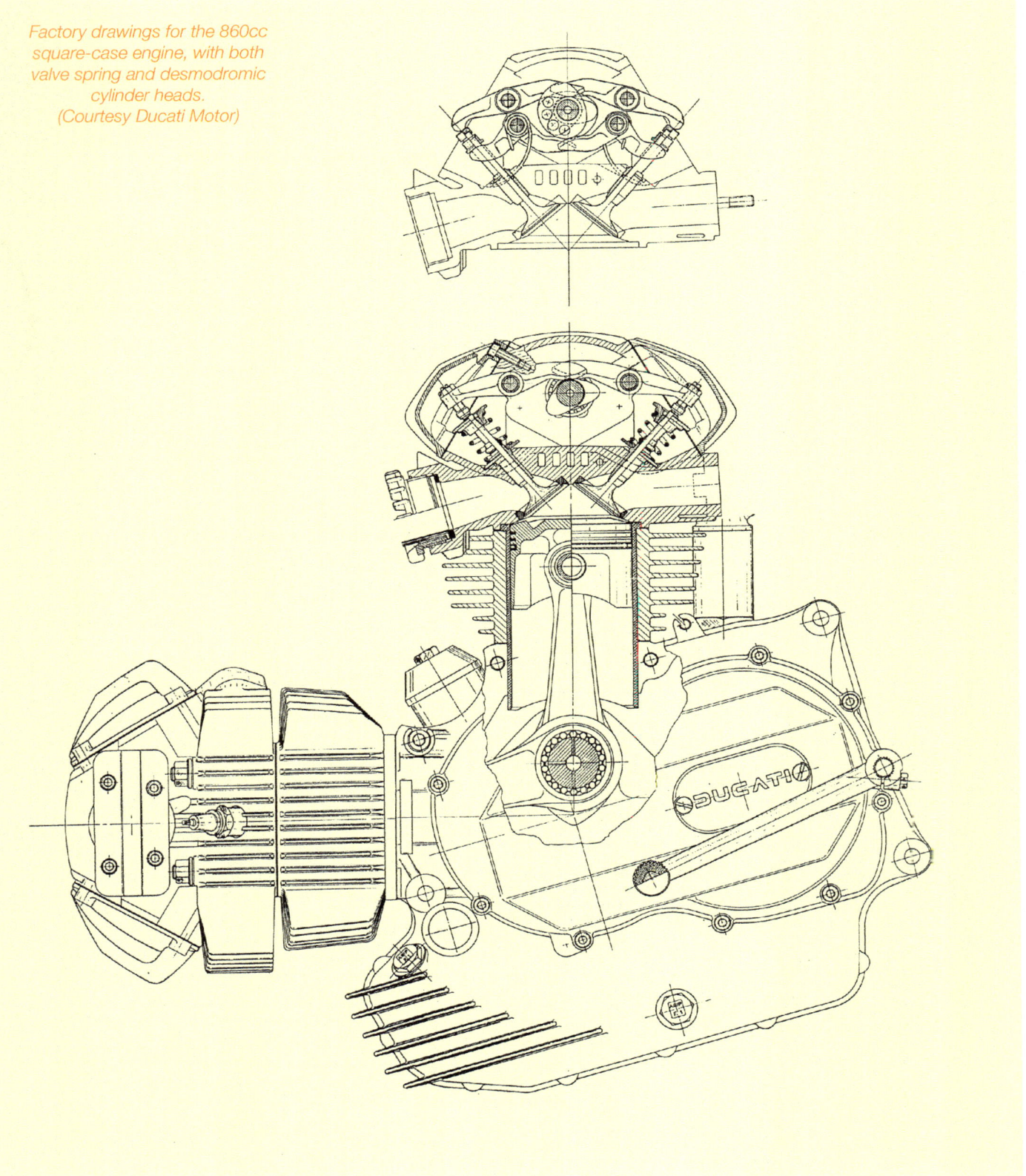

CHAPTER TWO

1975 – 860 GT, 860 GTE, 750 AND 900 SUPER SPORT

Although production of the new 860 GT commenced in September 1974, and 1671 examples were produced by December 31, it's convenient to consider all early 860s as 1975 models. There was no official model year in 1975 and, while the 860 entered production as the 750 finished, it wasn't generally available until 1975. The first official appearance in the UK was at the Racing and Sporting Show in January 1975. The transition from round-case to square-case was fast and smooth, and demonstrated the capacity of the factory to accommodate new designs.

To the casual observer the 860 GT looked to be a superficial styling exercise based on the 750, but there was much more to the 860 than merely an overbore. The entire machine was redesigned and restyled with the intention of making it more appealing to the US market. The engine also underwent considerable modification; firstly to simplify manufacture, and secondly to improve reliability and minimise maintenance. During 1973 there were further changes in management, and Milvio and Spairani were replaced by Ing. de Eccher. De Eccher's brief from his EFIM bosses was simple: he had to increase production and make the plant more profitable. Taglioni was instructed to redesign the 750 engine so that it was much less labour-intensive to manufacture and, by the end of 1973 when the 750 Super Sport was also displayed at the Milan Show, the writing was already on the wall for the round-case engine. It was the same for the singles that were due to be discontinued in favour of the ill-fated parallel twin.

860 GT and 860 GTE

While the earliest examples of the 750 GT, Sport, and 750 Super Sport could be categorised as pre-production, or limited production examples, this wasn't the case with the early 860. From the outset the 860 was designed for regular production. Almost as many 860s were produced in the four months from September 1974 as there had been 750 GTs in the previous seven months. De Eccher may have envisaged mass production of the 860, but this was unrealistic as the bike was still a complex twin with bevel gear-driven overhead camshafts. The problems with the early 860s were largely due to insufficient development.

The first series of 860 was remarkably consistent in specification. The new Giugiaro graphics were evident and, while the 860 received an unenthusiastic reception, the Giugiaro graphics were an artistic triumph that have stood the test of time.

Engine

There were a large number of updates for the 860 engine compared to the round-case 750, notably to the bevel-gear camshaft drive and lubrication system. While still drawing heavily on the 750 design, apart from the six-dog gearbox, most engine components were no longer interchangeable. The crankcase mouths were 100mm, to accept the 86mm cylinders, and the 860 engine cases were smoother, pressure

By the time it went into production, the 860 GT differed only slightly from the prototype. (Courtesy Ducati Motor)

Taglioni redesigned the engine cases of the 90-degree V-twin so they would complement the Giugiaro styling. (Courtesy Two Wheels)

die-castings, compared to the porous 750 type. Other small updates included slightly different length crankcase retaining bolts (M10x80mm and M10x70mm instead of M10x75mm). There were no matching crankcase assembly numbers, and engine numbers for the 860 GT and GTE began at DM860 850001. Numbers were stamped on

the rear of the left crankcase, with DM860 on the right crankcase.

The most noticeable feature of the 860 engine was the redesigned outer engine covers – alternator, clutch, bevel, and gearshift covers. Underneath the reshaped alternator cover was a new bevel-gear drive to the two vertical shafts.

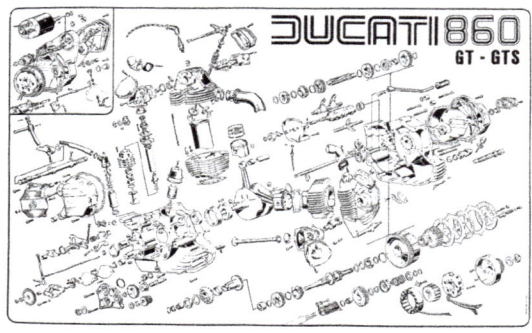

An exploded diagram of the 860 engine. In many respects it was similar to the 750, but had a redesigned bevel-gear camshaft drive.

Instead of running a bevel-gear directly from the crankshaft, there was now a keyed straight-cut gear driving two further spur gears mounted onto an outrigger plate. A 22-tooth gear drove the oil pump, while the other (24-tooth) drove two 36-tooth spur gears keyed to a 23-tooth bevel-gear. The right end of the crankshaft and two 36-tooth gears were supported on an aluminium outrigger plate securely bolted to the crankcase half by three 8x40mm and one 8x35mm bolts. The crankshaft spun in a 20x47x14mm roller bearing, and the two shafts in 15x42x13mm roller bearings. These two straight cut gears were keyed to bevels that drove the two shafts. It was a far easier system to assemble because the straight cut gear meshing was unaffected by sideways movement, and the two bevel-gear shafts could be set up individually. With the 750 system the bevel-gears were difficult to set up because altering one affected the mesh of another. The 860 set-up was superior, as crankshaft end play didn't affect the camshaft timing. As there was the outboard plate supporting the crankshaft and bevel drive-gears there was no longer an outside bearing incorporated in the alternator cover. The lower camshaft bevel-gears were also better located on the 860 engine because the retaining flanges used four, rather than two, M6x20mm screws. The lower bevel-gears were also easier to shim for bearing clearance as the bearings were retained inside the alloy housing instead of the separate steel housing that required a special tool for removal.

There were other improvements involved in the 860 redesign. The oil pump drive gear was no longer incorporated on the crankshaft, but was a keyed-on spur gear (machined with the crankshaft timing gear). As there was no central bevel gear with the ignition points drive, an oil filter was located between the bevel shafts. This was in addition to the plastic gauze strainer in the sump and the centrifugal sludge traps in the crank webs. Although only a bypass type, filtering a proportion of the oil on the way to the rear cylinder head, it was an improvement over the 750's arrangement. The oil filter was located by a black, pressed steel cover, and sealed with a rubber ring, but the gauze sump strainer was retained. Despite the wider crankcases, this was shorter than that

on the 750 and, although the parts list indicated a right-side crankcase plug, this was cast over on the 860. The oil pump was redesigned providing an increased oil flow (with a 51-tooth driving gear instead of 48-tooth), with wider (18mm) 11-tooth gears. The downside to the square-case engine was increased width and weight because of the extra gears in the camshaft drive assembly, and the provision for a wider alternator on the end of the crankshaft. Until engine number 851683 the alternator was still the narrow 150W three-wire type of the 750. From number 851684 the alternator was a 200W alternator two-wire type with a 30mm stator and much improved charge characteristics below 4000rpm. A new four-diode 18A regulator replaced the 750 two-diode 12A type. The date stipulated for the implantation of electrical updates was motorcycles manufactured after 20 May 1975, but this is confusing as engine numbers were certainly beyond 851684 by this date.

For some reason, possibly to reduce engine length allowing a slightly shorter wheelbase, the cylinders and con-rods were shorter. The con-rod eye-to-eye length was reduced by 5mm to 145mm, providing a rod/stroke ratio of 1.95:1 with the 74.4mm stroke. The shorter con-rod helped increase mid-range power slightly, but with an increase in piston acceleration. The con-rods were forged, as on the 750, with a single rib around the big-end eye, but were less 'blocky' in shape as the gudgeon pin diameter was reduced to 20x59mm (from 22mm).

Although retaining the same 32/70 primary drive ratio of the 1974 750 GT, the primary gears were new. The crankshaft primary gear bolted to a new flywheel that incorporated the Ducati Elettrotecnica electronic ignition magnets, with the ignition stator located on the crankcase inside the flywheel. The flywheel on the 860 was much lighter than that of the 750. As on the final 750, the clutch drum used two 25x47x12mm bearings with a 1.9mm spacer and Seeger ring, but the clutch plates were new. The inner driving plate featured outward-facing bent tags, the seven friction plates were thinner, and a 1.5mm spacer was incorporated between the inner and outer clutch drums. The outside pressure plate was also new, but the six clutch springs were unchanged from the 750. The clutch actuation system running through the main shaft was as before, but the two long rods were now 113.5mm instead of 110mm.

This arrangement of clutch plates was only fitted until engine number 851193. After engine number 851194 there was no longer a spacer fitted between the inner and outer clutch drum, and the inner drum was deeper. Only one of the

The 860 GT air cleaners included metal air boxes. An electric start was integral to the design. (Courtesy Two Wheels)

previous friction plates was retained, this the inner plate with the inner tags facing outwards. The friction plates reverted to those of the 750 and the driving plate with bent tags moved to the outside with the tags facing inwards. The pressure plate was also the same as that on the 750, but the six 8.4x1.6mm washers underneath the clutch springs were omitted. This clutch modification was not as successful as anticipated, and altered again from engine number 852178 to the same specification as the 860 GTS. This saw a return to a similar clutch drum bearing setup of the first 750 GT. The clutch drum bearings went back to one 25x47x12 and one 25x52x15 with the same clutch plate arrangement as used after engine number 851194. Unlike the early 750 GT, the 25.5x36x2.7mm spacer underneath the clutch housing was retained.

The displacement increase for the 860 over the 750 was achieved with a 6mm overbore using 86mm 9:1 AE Borgo pistons. These still used three rings, but were a slipper type similar to the Mondial pistons of the 750 Sport. The valve sizes (40mm inlet and 36mm exhaust) were unchanged, and the cylinder head castings were new, with an additional oil drain channel below the camshaft bearing support. There were new camshafts for the 860, with different timing and profile to the 750 GT. While the timing figures were more moderate, with less duration and overlap, valve lift was increased. 860 and 750 camshafts weren't interchangeable because the camshaft keyway was located in a different position. Following on from the last 750 GTs, the valve adjustment was now by screw and lock nut. On the 860 GT, the left-side camshaft bearing support housing was rectangular, in keeping with the angular engine covers, and had '860' engravings. The cylinder head was still sealed with O-rings, but the two smaller ones changed to 203s from 107s and the three larger bushes contained larger (8mm) oil passages.

The Dell'Orto PHF 32 AD/AS carburettors were similar to those used on the 750 Sport, with the rear cylinder featuring an identical intake manifold to the front. As with all Dell'Orto carburettors of this period, the float bowls were polished and had aluminium fuel junction banjos. The 860 GT also featured an improved air filtration system over that of the 750 GT, with less flexible air hoses to the two metal filter boxes. The exhaust system was also new for the 860, the early models still using single thickness 36mm header pipes, but with angular Lafranconi mufflers. The right Lafranconi muffler didn't include a kick-start recess, and the front exhaust header pipe was wired and sealed.

The ignition system on the 860 was the Ducati Elettrotecnica system that had been intended for the 750 but never installed because of the reliability problems experienced when fitted to the 500 Grand Prix racers during 1971. The stator was mounted directly on the inner left crankcase, near the main bearing, and was susceptible to failure. Two transducers under the tank provided the sparks, now with black high tension leads, but still with the rubber KLG spark plug caps. Champion L88A spark plugs were specified for the 860 GT/GTE. The ignition system provided a fairly abrupt advance, with maximum advance of 28 degrees ±2 degrees from 1700rpm (±300rpm). The maximum advance was 35-38 degrees.

On early 860s the ignition stop relay inside the headlight shell, grounding the two green cables from the ignition transducers, was problematic. From engine number 851684 an improved engine stop relay was fitted inside the headlight shell. One feature of the earlier electrical system was the ability to run the engine without a battery, without modification to the electrical system. The improved engine stop relay still allowed the engine to run without a battery, but the two (green) relay wires had to be disconnected.

In view of forthcoming US legislation the gearshift was moved to the left-hand side of the engine. This wasn't a particularly neat arrangement as the selector mechanism was still retained in the right-side cover, as with the 750. The left-side shift was obtained through two splined levers and a rod running behind the engine, with some of the 750's gear change precision lost. Along with the left-side gearshift conversion there was a neutral indicator switch mounted behind the selector box. A 16-tooth countershaft was fitted to all 1974-built bikes, along with a 40-tooth rear sprocket and

108-link ⅝x⅜in Renold chain. Early in 1975 this was revised, with 15- and 38-toothed sprockets and a 106-link Renold chain.

Unlike the 750 GT, an electric starter was integral to the concept of the 860, but it wasn't until January 1975 that electric start versions were produced. Models with an electric start carried the designation 860 GTE. A kick-start was still fitted, with a 335mm shaft. The electric start mechanism was also the same as for the 750 GT (E), except for the inclusion of a 5mm tie rod to activate the starter motor. A 1.2 horsepower Marelli electric motor turned the engine via chain-driven 11- and 21-toothed sprockets and a 38-tooth Regina Extra chain. The starter was keyed to a gear that meshed with another on the flywheel. It wasn't an entirely trouble free system and underwent further modification during 1975. The GTE used a larger Yuasa B68-12 36Ah battery. Although the 860 GTE was an important part of the 860 line-up, problems with the starter switch burning out and a delay in production until 1975 resulted in most 860s being kick-start only (1821 kick-start and 1166 electric start).

Chassis

Although the prototype 860 was derived from the 750 GT, by the time the production 860 was finalised it had a completely new frame and running

Most early 860s were without an electric start and had a single front disc brake.
(Courtesy Two Wheels)

gear. Frame numbers began at DM860S 850001, stamped on the steering head with a new frame homologation number DGM 13715 OM. There was a silencer homologation plate on the right-hand side between the two engine mounts, mounted with the top towards the engine, as with the later 750s. Because of the new frame and silencers this had new homologation numbers of DM860S E3 9R-13716. The black-painted frame was redesigned to provide for a considerably narrower fuel tank and seat than the 750 GT, and was 216mm at the seat's widest point, the same as the 750 Sport and Super Sport.

After experience gained with the 1973 Imola 750 racers The 860 frame was shorter, at 1660mm, than that of the 750 GT, and the swingarm featured eccentric pivot chain adjusters instead of the Seeley type. The swingarm retained the 6mm oil nipple of the 750, and the chain guard was black-painted steel. The front frame downtubes were bowed, with additional curved braces between the downtubes and the more rounded top tubes. The bolt tabs on the front downtubes were flattened and the steering head angle increased to 31 degrees. The usual Neiman steering head lock was fitted, and the rear subframe included a raised section at the back, following the shape of the seat. On the US versions a side stand was mounted on the left front downtube.

All 860 GTs and GTEs were fitted with a 38mm Ceriani front fork. This had polished aluminium fork legs, with 608mm fork tubes and 525mm fork springs, which were longer than those fitted to the 1974 750 GT. There were black 'Ceriani' decals on both fork legs. As with the 750 GTs fitted with Ceriani forks, the upper and lower triple clamps were painted black and the headlamp brackets were black-painted steel. The 280mm, undrilled, cast-iron front disc brake used a single, forward-mounted Brembo P2F08N caliper, with a plastic cover and two bleed nipples. The front 15.8mm master cylinder was without a clear fluid reservoir, and the lever included an eccentric adjuster. The rubber brake hose went to a junction on the lower triple clamp where there was a brake light pressure switch with a rubber cover. Dual disc brakes were always an option and, from 1975, were fitted as standard to most electric start 860s. The rear brake was the 750 GT's Grimeca 200mm single leading-shoe drum brake, with a 350mm long brake rod attached to the swingarm. The rear suspension was Marzocchi, the 320mm shock absorbers with black plastic covers with red decals, and chrome-plated springs.

The first 860 GTs had a seat without a passenger strap. There was also no indent for the kick-start in the Lafranconi muffler. (Courtesy Two Wheels)

US models also had Lucas reflectors on a plate mounted on the top shock absorber bolt. Similar reflectors were mounted on each headlight retaining bolt.

The wheels were 18in front and rear, the rims chromed steel WM3x18in rims 40-spoke Radaelli Aimon Sport No 2262C. The silver-painted spokes were 4/3.5x166 on the front and 4/3.5x138 on the rear, 20 curved at 85 degrees and 20 curved at 90 degrees. The same sized tires were fitted front and rear, Pirelli Gordon MT18 or 3.50H18 Metzeler Block C66 on US models.

All the bodywork was new for the 860, the angular steel 18 litre fuel tank located by two 8mm rubber mounts to the frame. This included plastic 'DUCATI' badges on each side, Brev Orlandi fuel taps, and green 6x13mm plastic fuel lines with zinc-plated spring clips. The seat hinged on the left-hand side of the rear subframe, and was located by a lock on the right. At the rear of the kicked up seat was the name 'DUCATI' in the new Giugiaro lettering. 1974-built examples didn't include a seat strap, but sometime during 1975 the seat included a strap. The redesigned steel side covers were located by four M6x42 screws with spacers and also had plastic '860' badges. Angular painted steel mudguards completed the styling effort. All the initial examples were painted metallic orange, or bronze, with green, blue, black, and red following in smaller numbers during 1975.

Ducati went to some effort to improve many components that had come under criticism on the 750 and to meet new US standards. Only the US-style high and wide handlebar was fitted to the 860 GT, with the wires through the bars. The clutch lever and choke assembly incorporated a new CEV switch block, and clutch cable adjustment was by two metal rings. The CEV switch block differed between US and European 860s. European light switches were blue, and the high/low beam switch black. US 860s had a black light switch, blue main beam, low beam and parking light switch, black horn button, and blue headlamp flasher. On the right-hand side the single cable throttle assembly also included another CEV switch block with a black engine kill switch, black indicator switch, and a red electric start button. The right-side switch block was prone to burning out on the first 860 GTEs, but modifications during 1975 seemingly cured that problem. Early 860 GTs had hard plastic handgrips, soon changed for the usual rubber Verlicchi. A choke was incorporated on the left switch block, and had an alloy lever.

Turn signal indicators were standard on the 860 GT, the round Aprilia type fitted to US versions with 21W bulbs, and new rectangular Aprilia indicators with 15W bulbs on 860s for the rest of the world. During 1975 the square-shaped 15W Aprilia indicators were standardized to the 21W round type. There were also two types of headlamp fitted for the two different markets; US 860 GTs featuring a sealed-beam headlight (without parking light) with a different headlamp rim and headlamp retaining system. European 860 GTs included the 170mm Aprilia JOD Duplo 55/60W halogen headlamp of the 750 Sport and Super Sport (with 3W parking light). Inside the headlamp shell was a relay for the headlamp, a flasher unit for the indicators, an engine stop relay, and a two-tone horn device. The Aprilia fusebox was now a five-fuse type, located under the seat next to the regulator.

The 860 dashboard was similar to the final 750 GT type, with Smiths instruments, a 150mph (or 250km/h) speedometer on the left. The trip meter was reset via a knob which protruded through the dashboard. On the right was the Smiths tachometer (redlined at 7000rpm) and in between the instruments were five warning lights (although Veglia Borletti instruments were also stipulated in the parts list, most 860s, if not all, had Smiths instruments) – a red generator light, white for lights, blue for high beam, yellow for indicators, and a green neutral indicator. On the lower right of these warning lights was the two-volume horn switch, a low volume for town and a higher volume for the country. The two-volume Belli model 90, type B horn was mounted under the fuel tank. Under the tank on the left was the three-position ignition switch. Two different CEV, black metal taillight brackets were fitted to 860s, both using the larger CEV 9350 lens.

The footpeg rubbers, mounted on folding

During 1975 the 860 GT was offered with a lower seat option. Some of these later 860 GTs had electric start and dual front disc brakes. (Courtesy Ducati Motor)

pegs, were the same as those on the 750 GT, but there were new frame mounts that located the pedals further apart and forward. The conversion of the cable-operated rear drum brake to right-side operation was achieved by using a rod running below the swingarm, locating the brake lever directly underneath the exhaust pipe. During 1975 this shaft was modified, the cable connection was splined onto the shaft instead of being a one-piece unit. There was a rubber foot pad on the brake lever, and the brake light switch was still incorporated in the cable on the left-hand side. Another update during 1975 was the option of a lower seat similar to that of the 500 GTL parallel twin.

Although history has been unkind to the 860 GT, some of its misfortune was due to unfortunate timing. Its release coincided with a slump in motorcycle sales, particularly in the US, and this resulted in stockpiles of the 750, as well as the 860, during 1975. Other Italian manufacturers were also affected by this recession, notably Laverda, Benelli, and Moto Guzzi. Of the 5977 motorcycles Ducati manufactured in 1975, 1360 were 860 GTs and many of these remained unsold into 1976. Total 860 GT/GTE production was 2987, all manufactured between September 1974 and July 1975. Some 860 GTEs would be converted in 860 GTSs during 1976 and, as there was considerable overlap with the 860 GTS, engine and frame numbers continued to around 853600.

In the United States controversy erupted early in 1975 when the Indian Motorcycle Corporation displayed the Indian 860 at the Anaheim Trade Show. West Coast Ducati Distributor Bob Blair was incensed, claiming the Indian was a Ducati 860 GT with a larger rear wheel and new fuel tank, seat, and side covers. After Ducati's vice chairman Cosimo Calcagnile intervened it was ascertained the Indian 860 was built out of spare parts by Leopoldo Tartarini who had purchased 50 engines with the proviso they couldn't be sold in the US The issue was eventually resolved and the Indian 860 didn't eventuate.

Another publicity picture of the 860 GT with the lower seat, this time with a single front disc brake. (Courtesy Ducati Motor)

1975 860 GT distinguishing features
(from engine number DM860 850001-853600 approx., frame number DM860S 850001-853600 approx.)

Engine
New crankcase castings
Longer kick-start shaft than 750
Gear selection still in right cover but with crossover shaft behind the crankcase
Neutral indicator switch on selector shaft
Angular outer engine covers
New primary drive and clutch
Clutch updated after engine number 851194 and 852178
Spring fitted inside engine breather tube
Oil filter incorporated in right crankcase between cylinders
Shorter gauze crankcase oil strainer and no right crankcase plug
86mm Borgo pistons and shorter cylinders
145mm forged con-rods with 20mm gudgeon pin
New cylinder head castings with two oil drain channels
200W alternator from engine number 851684
Improved ignition stop relay after engine number 851684
Ducati Elettrotecnica ignition
KLG spark plug caps with black ignition leads
Left-side gearshift
Dell'Orto PHF 32A carburettors
Single-walled 36mm exhaust header pipes
Lafranconi mufflers, right-side without kick-start recess

Chassis
New frame DM860S with DGM 13715 OM homologation number
Swingarm with eccentric pivot chain adjustment
38mm Ceriani front fork with polished alloy fork legs and black triple clamps
280mm Brembo 08 front disc brake (twin disc optional)
Brembo front master cylinder with polished alloy lever and eccentric adjuster
Rubber brake hoses with metal caliper connection for front brake
320mm Marzocchi rear shock absorbers with three preload positions, black plastic spring covers, and chrome-plated springs
18in steel-rimmed Radaelli wheels front and rear
Smiths instruments
Dashboard with five warning lights
City/country horn
Alloy choke lever on left handlebar
CEV handlebar switches
Aprilia turn signals (two types)
Angular shaped 18-litre steel fuel tank and side covers with plastic badges
Kicked up seat without strap on early examples

Some 860 GTs were produced as police motorcycles. This example is a hybrid with an 860 engine in a 750 frame. (Courtesy Ducati Motor)

750 and 900 Super Sport

When the 860 GT was introduced in late 1974 it was intended to replace the entire 750 line-up, including the Sport and Super Sport. Race replicas were no longer considered economically viable, but another limited production run of Super Sports was undertaken early in 1975. When asked by the author how this came about, given the known animosity between Taglioni and de Eccher, Taglioni replied: "The 1975 Super Sport was produced at the request of various distributors, but it was my idea to base it on the earlier 750 Super Sport because we knew this chassis would work for racing." The production run of less than 500 Super Sports (750 and 900) began in April to May 1975, and they were amongst the last motorcycles built without regard to emissions, noise, and left-side gearshift requirements. As the frame number sequence was shared, and numbers for each model not consecutive, the 750 and 900 was

obviously built in concurrent batches. Most of these Super Sports were destined for Australia, Canada, South Africa, and Italy, where they were eligible for production racing. By June 1975 the 900 SS was already advertised in Australia, and it made its first appearance in England at the Earls Court Motorcycle Show in August. One was on the HGB Motorcycles stand for £1999, and another on the Coburn and Hughes stand. An amalgam of the earlier 750 and new 860, the 1975 Super Sport was one of the finest of all production Ducati motorcycles. It was also a stylistic triumph. Ducati doesn't always get it right with its styling, but it certainly did with the 1975 Super Sport.

Engine

Although the 1975 Super Sport was based on the 1974 version, the engine was ostensibly that of the 'square-case' 860 GT. The crankcases included a new designation and number sequence: 'DM750.1' for the 750 SS; and 'DM860.1' for the 900 SS, stamped on the right crankcase half. The 750 Super Sport continued the number sequence of the earlier 750 SS (starting at 075412 and ending at 075661), while the 900 SS had a new sequence beginning at 086001 and ending at 086250. Both continued the limited edition '.1' designation, and the crankcases featured a pair of matching four digit numbers stamped underneath, near the wire lead seal. The crankcase mouths were the same size for the 750 and 900, with the 750 barrels including a thicker sleeve.

But for desmodromic cylinder heads and a different crankshaft and pistons, internally the engine was identical to that of the 860 GT. The 750 SS also used a 20mm gudgeon pin, slightly shorter at 52mm. Unlike the 1974 750 SS that had special con-rods machined from billet steel, the con-rod was the forged 860 type, but with a dual strengthening rib around the big end. At around 440g each, these rods were slightly heavier than the 1974 version, but they were stronger. The three-ring Super Sport pistons were also supplied by AE Borgo, the 900 86mm pistons providing a compression ratio of 9.5:1, and the 750 80mm pistons 9.65:1. The 900 SS

The 1975 900 Super Sport successfully blended the rounded style of the earlier Super Sport with the angular 860 engine cases.

The 900 Super Sport camshaft bearing housings didn't include '860' markings.

pistons had a noticeably higher dome than those fitted to the 860 GT. The cylinder heads were shared with the 860 (with two oil channels under the bearing support), but with the desmodromic valve layout of the 1974 750 SS. As with the 1974 Super Sport the opening and closing rockers were polished on 1975 models. The camshafts provided identical valve timing figures, but because of the revised bevel-drive system the keyway was in a different position. The 750 and 900 Super Sport cylinder heads looked identical, although the 750 retained the round-case '750' camshaft bearing supports and a smaller squish band, while the 900 had the angular 860 GT bearing supports (without '860' lettering).

All 1975 Super Sports were fitted with the later 860 200W two-wire alternator, and finned four-diode, 18A regulator. Ignition was provided by two transducers mounted on the top frame tube, firing Champion L81 spark plugs through black ignition leads and the KLG spark plug caps. The clutch was the 860 GT

Dell'Orto PHM 40A carburettors fed the desmodromic cylinder heads. The early carburettors had bell mouths with wire mesh, polished aluminium float bowls, and metal banjos.

type fitted after engine number 851194, with two identical clutch housing bearings. The Super Sport included an additional 25.5x32x1.9mm spacer with a Seeger ring between the two bearings. The inner clutch drum was narrower on the 1975 Super Sport (43mm) than the 860, but the other clutch components were the same (not as in the parts catalogue). The gearshift was on the right, and all 1975 Super Sports were kick-start only, the lever designed to clear the gearshift. This kick-start lever was specific to 1975 Super Sports only. Because the Super Sport still featured a right-side gearshift, the 860 clutch cover included a plug for the crossover gearshift shaft exit.

The Dell'Orto PHM 40 A carburettors, jetting, and welded steel intake manifolds were identical to those of the 1974 750 Super Sport. Generally the carburettor bodies were smooth with no provision for a choke but, as supplies of the early carburettors dwindled, some Super Sports came with a later type carburettor, with the choke mounting cast in the body. The plastic bell mouths also featured wire gauze filters. The engine breather was the same rubber bellows system as on the 1974 750 SS (and some 1974 750 Sports).

Whereas the 860 GT had Lafranconi mufflers, the Conti exhaust system from the 1974 750 Super Sport featured on the 1975 Super Sport. The Conti mufflers had the same short brackets but, instead of four 'M'-type clamps, there were two, smaller diameter 'R'-type clamps at the front. The single-walled header pipes were new, to clear the wider outer covers, and the left-side angled outwards to provide access to the oil filler.

With its open carburettors and free flowing exhaust the 1975 Super Sport (particularly the 900), provided significantly more performance than the 750 or 860. It was no surprise, then, that this model was so competitive in production racing.

Chassis

As it was a limited edition model, the 1975 Super Sport carried its frame number sequence over from the 1974 750 Super Sport. Probably in order to use the previous homologation number (DGM 11871 OM) both 900 Super Sports and 750 Super Sports shared the same frame number sequence, beginning at DM750 SS 075412. Some frames featured only five numbers, missing the '0'. These frames were mostly around 75460-75510. There were also some later frames without the '0'. Most frames without the additional '0' appeared on 750s, as did most of the first 70 frame numbers. This

The 1975 750 Super Sport was very similar to the 900, but was distinguished by a sliver fairing with b'ue decals. (Courtesy Ducati Motor)

doesn't indicate that the 750s were built before the 900s, however, as the frame numbers were stamped after painting and stacked in racks. As it was for the engines, frame selection for the assembly line was random.

The Verlicchi-built, silver-painted frame was similar to that of the 1974 750 SS, but with different brackets for the rear master cylinder and ignition transducers, but appears to have been built on a different jig. The basic frame dimensions were not identical because the underneath fuel tank and rear mudguard were shaped differently, and not interchangeable with the 1974 type. The frame-mounted headlight and instrument support was also painted silver. The right-side silencer homologation plate carried the numbers DM750 SS E3-9R-11872. The silver and blue bodywork was patterned on that of the 1974 750 Super Sport, although the 20-litre fibreglass fuel tank no longer included the clear strip 'fuel gauge'. The front mudguard had four mounting points on each side, and the black and white 'DUCATI' lettering on the tank was the new Giugiaro-type. The rear mudguard included a black plastic circular guide under the seat for the wiring harness. The side cover decals were black and white, and a black and white 'DESMO' decal was placed on each side of the lower fairing and at the rear of the seat. The 900 featured a blue fairing (also painted blue inside) with silver stripes, while the 750 fairing was silver (also on the inside) with blue stripes. The Ballanti Roberto plexiglass screen was 1.6mm thick, and was inconsistent as to the height. The example used for publicity hac an extremely low screen while others were higher.

Three blue stripes went along the front fender, fuel tank and seat. There was no provision for frame-mounted turn signals.

Unlike the 860 GT the front suspension was Marzocchi: the 38mm centre-axle fork with black fork legs, four mounts for the front mudguard, and forward mount Brembo brake calipers. The rear twin Marzocchi shock absorbers were 310mm and similar to the 1974 version, with black springs and top rubber covers, but featured five preload positions. The 40-spoke, 18in WM3 4777 Borrani wheels and Metzeler 3.50V18 Block C7 Racing tires were identical to those used on the 1974 750 Super Sport. The flared rims were still the early Borrani type. There was no change to the 16- and 40-tooth final drive sprockets, but there was a new 104-link Regina ASA 50 chain this year.

While the frame and suspension were very similar to those on the 1974 Super Sport, the

On the 1975 Super Sport the wheels were still the early Borrani, but the brake discs were drilled, and the brake calipers Brembo with smooth bodies.

Brembo braking system was new. The twin front discs now measured 280x6.35mm, and were drilled with spiral patterns of seven holes. The Brembo brake calipers were also different to those on the 860 GT as they had smooth bodies and no plastic pad cover. The pads were slightly thinner than on the regular Brembo caliper. Also unique for 1975 was a Brembo front master cylinder without a clear reservoir, the body having the usual mirror mount ground off. Not only was the Brembo system functionally superior to the Scarab, the master cylinder design was improved because the lever no longer held the piston in place. Brake hoses were rubber, a single 210mm hose joining the master cylinder to the junction on the lower triple clamp, with two 360mm rubber hoses and metal pipe connecting the brake calipers. The brake pressure switch (with rubber cover) was at the junction on the lower triple clamp.

At the rear was a slightly smaller diameter

drilled disc than for 1974 (229x6.35mm). The Brembo master cylinder was located behind the left-side cover, with a 370mm rubber hose. The brake pressure stop switch (with rubber cover) protruded underneath the rear mudguard and, although the rear Brembo caliper had a new aluminium support plate, the rear wheel cush drive assembly was unchanged.

Apart from the more angular Brembo black front brake lever, most equipment was the same as for the 1974 Super Sport. This included the Verlicchi clip-on handlebars with Allen bolts and welded nuts, Verlicchi handgrips, and earlier (rounder) black clutch lever and support. Also shared with the 1974 Super Sport were the solid steel footpegs with same $7/16$in UNF thread. The throttle was the earlier Tommaselli Daytona 2C with the throttle stop screw on the top and small rubber cover. Although the gearshift and rear brake set-up was identical, the 1975 Super Sport had new gearshift and brake levers to accommodate the wider outer engine covers. The linkages retained the clevis fork with 7mm pins.

Instead of sharing the ancillary equipment of the 860 GT, the 1975 Super Sport was more of a carryover from 1974. From the earlier Super Sport came Smiths instruments and instrument panel, although for the UK a 150mph speedometer was now specified. The speedometer was on the right, with the tachometer on the left, and the horn was a single Belli, not two-tone. Apart from the

The 1975 Super Sport Brembo master cylinder had a solid body and the mirror mounts ground off. The angular brake lever didn't match the clutch lever.

As on the 1974 Super Sport the rear master cylinder was located under the left-hand side cover. For 1975 this was Brembo, with a new bracket.

The 1975 Super Sport retained the earlier clutch lever and CEV light and horn switch.

The rear disc brake of the 1975 Super Sport with Brembo brake caliper. Many components were specific to this model, including the Marzocchi shock absorbers.

Also identical to the 1974 Super Sport was the Aprilia instrument panel and Smiths instruments.

The author's 1975 900 Super Sport (engine 086065 and frame 075542). The 1975 Super Sport was undoubtedly one of the finest motorcycles ever built by Ducati.

electronic ignition, the electrical system was that of the 1974 Super Sport. A four-pin, two-position ignition switch was positioned between the seat and fuel tank on the left-hand side, and the Aprilia fusebox under the seat contained four fuses. The Aprilia high/low beam/horn switch on the left handlebar was also straight off the earlier Super Sport. All 1975 Super Sports were manufactured before May 20, the cut-off date for the fitting of a revised engine stop relay under the fuel tank instead of in the headlight shell. Both the Aprilia 170mm 'JOD' Duplo 55/60W halogen headlamp with chrome-plated shell, and steel, silver-painted

European specification CEV taillight were shared with the 1974 Super Sport. Like the 1974 SS, the CEV taillight bracket had a longer extension than that fitted to the 750 GT. They also had 'CEV' pressed into the base.

Although not produced in great numbers, or widely available, the 1975 Super Sport was a very significant model for Ducati. It continued the tradition of limited edition race replicas and consolidated Ducati's position as one of the leading manufacturers of sporting motorcycles. Despite Laverda improving its 1000 3C in 1975, the 900 SS was the leader in the world of superbikes.

1975 750 and 900 Super Sport distinguishing features (from engine number DM750.1 075412-075661; DM860.1 086001-086250, frame numbers DM750SS 075412-075911)

Engine

860 crankcases with DM860.1 or DM750.1 number sequence
Forged con-rods with dual strengthening rib and 20mm gudgeon pin
Three-ring Borgo pistons
Desmodromic camshafts
Polished valve rockers
900 SS camshaft bearing supports without '860' engraving
750 SS camshaft bearing supports as for round-case 750
200W alternator and finned four-diode 18A regulator
Champion L81 spark plugs, black high tension leads and KLG plug caps
Second type 860 clutch
Narrower inner clutch drum than 860
Dell'Orto PHM 40A carburettors with wire gauze bell mouths and polished float bowls
Some carburettors with smooth bodies and no choke attachment
Right-side gearshift
Straight kick-start lever
Exhaust system with Conti mufflers with short brackets
Two 'M' and two 'R' Conti clamps
New single walled exhaust header pipes
Engine breather with rubber bellows reservoir

Chassis

Silver-painted 750 SS frame with 750 SS 075 frame number sequence
Some frames with five-digit frame numbers
Silver and blue fibreglass bodywork similar to 1974 750 SS
20-litre fibreglass fuel tank with black and white 'DUCATI' decals
Rear mudguard included a wiring harness guide under the seat

900 SS with blue fairing and silver stripes
750 SS with silver fairing and blue stripes
Plexiglass screen located with 7 slot head screws
No turn signals
38mm Marzocchi fork with black fork legs, Brembo connection and four-bolt front mudguard
310mm Marzocchi rear shock absorbers with five position black springs and top rubber covers
18in WM3 4777 Borrani wheels and Metzeler 3.50V18 Elock C7 racing tires
280mm drilled (7-hole pattern) front brake discs and Brembo 08 shaved brake calipers
Rubber brake hoses with metal caliper connection for front brake
Front Brembo master cylinder without clear reservoir and mirror mounts ground off
229mm drilled rear disc with Brembo 08 shaved brake caliper
Verlicchi clip-on handlebars with Allen bolts and welded nuts
Verlicchi handgrips
Older style round black clutch lever and support
Chrome Aprilia high/low beam/horn switch on the left handlebar
Tommaselli Daytona 2C with throttle stop screw on the top and small rubber cover
Solid steel footpegs with $7/16$in UNF thread
Smiths instruments and three light instrument panel (UK 150mph speedometer)
Four-pin, two-position ignition switch was positioned between the seat and fuel tank.
Four-fuse Aprilia fusebox
Aprilia 170mm 'JOD' Duplo 55/60W halogen headlamp with chrome-plated shell
Steel silver-painted European specification CEV taillight bracket

Racing the 1975 Super Sport

As the Super Sport's raison d'être was production racing, it was no surprise to see it immediately take to the track. Most of the production run went to Australia, and many were raced. The first victory for the 900 SS was at Bathurst in April 1975, where Kenny Blake won the 20-lap unlimited production race. This machine was a special factory-supplied round-case 860, and it was a convincing win ahead of a field of Kawasaki 900s. A few months later the production 900 Super Sport appeared, just in time for the annual Castrol Six-hour production race. This was the first time that the Super Sport was eligible for this race, and several examples were entered. John Warrian very nearly won, his engine failing with only 23 minutes left while in the lead. Over the next three years victory always eluded the 900 SS in the Six-hour race. The 1976 Super Sport was not available in time for the

1976 event, and the field included seven 1975 900 SSs and one 750 SS. This year Danny Oakhill and Ross Pink finished third, and were leading before their rear tyre disintegrated. While always in contention in the Six-hour race, after a strong fourth in 1977, the best result for the 1975 900 SS was Warrian's second place in 1978. The last time it could run under the four-year limit, this time Warrian was teamed with Terry Kelly. Warrian made amends in the Surfers Paradise Three-hour race shortly afterwards, teaming with Ron Boulden to take an easy victory.

The 1975 900 SS was also successful in other production events. In March 1976 Greg Johnson won the Adelaide Three-hour unlimited production race, and Dennis Noyes and John Knowles took a victory in the BFRC 700-kilometre event at Cadwell Park in July 1976. Malcolm Moffatt also won the production class at the 1976 North West 200 on a 1975 900 SS.

Below: John Warrian very nearly provided the 900 Super Sport a maiden victory in the 1975 Australian Six-Hour production race.

Right: Only minutes from victory the 900's engine expired. A dejected Warrian pushes the bike back to the pits. (Courtesy Two Wheels)

Warrian rode the 1975 900 Super Sport until 1978. Here he is on his way to victory at Surfers Paradise, still with Castrol 6-Hour plates, testing the ground clearance to the maximum. (Courtesy Two Wheels)

CHAPTER THREE

1976 – 860 GTS

In September 1975 Franco Zauibouri replaced Cristiano de Eccher as Ducati's general manager. Like so many EFIM managers Zauibouri had no direct motorcycle experience. He came from an agricultural engineering background but endeavoured to make some amends by enlisting the support of Taglioni. Taglioni had earlier refused to become involved in the development of the parallel twin, but Zauibouri now agreed to the development of the Pantah as the next generation middleweight. By August 1975 860 GTs were stockpiled, but all markets were clamouring for

The prototype 860 GTS featured the 860 GT's rectangular turn signals and slightly different decals. (Courtesy Two Wheels)

the limited production Super Sport. At Taglioni's request Zauibouri also allowed the 860 GTS restyling and an update to the 750 and 900 Super Sport so it could meet registration requirements anywhere in the world. Initial plans called for the 900 Super Sport to be a 1976 model, and Ducati went as far as to print an owners' manual in February 1976 that mentioned a 1976 version, seven months before actual series production. But 1976 was another year characterised by poor management decisions. Ducati saw its future at this time with smaller capacity motorcycles, and most 1976 production centred on the 125 Regolarità enduro and 350 and 500 parallel twins. These proved disastrous models but, although 1976 wasn't a good year for the bevel-drive twin, with the 900 Super Sport set for series production as a 1977 model the prospects looked more promising.

860 GTS

In response to the poor sales of the 860 GT and GTE, the Giugiaro 860 GT design was restyled during 1975. A prototype 860 GTS was displayed during May and differed in small details to the

eventual production version. Production of the 860 GT was discontinued in July 1975 and, from September, it was replaced by the 860 GTS. 1975-built 860 GTs continued to be available, and many were modified with a lower and flatter seat. Some were also fitted with 860 GTS fuel tanks but they were otherwise unchanged. Production of the 860 GTS commenced after September 1975, and although 570 were produced in 1975 it wasn't readily available until 1976 and it is convenient to consider the 860 GTS a 1976 model.

Engine

All 860 GTSs were electric start and the engine unit was shared with the 860 GTE. There was considerable overlap in engine numbers between the 860 GTE and GTS as early 860 GTSs featured standard 860 GTE engines. Motors were obviously built and stockpiled during 1975 with 860 GTS engine numbers beginning around 852000. Around engine number 853000 some specific 860 GTS updates were incorporated, also fitted to later 860 GTs. As all GTSs were manufactured after 20 May 1975 (engine number 851684) they featured the updated ignition and electrical system.

An early 860 GTS (frame number 853030). All 860 GTSs had electric start and dual front disc brakes. Early bikes like this one had decals on the fuel tank.

Updates extended from the revised location of the right-side internal gearshift lever, now held by a Seeger ring instead of a screw, to the gearbox that featured a new 22-tooth 5th gear on the layshaft, and updated layshaft. In an effort to improve the kick-start ratio, the kick-start shaft gear was changed from a 35-tooth to 36-tooth for the 860 GTS. The 860 GTS clutch was different again to the updated 860 GT type (from engine number 851194), with a 750 inner clutch drum and new clutch housing. As with the 860 GT, after engine number 852177 there was another new clutch drum with new bearings. The electric start motor and gearing were also altered for the GTS. This included a new motor (MT65/B-08/12/S) with a 15-tooth sprocket and 40-link starting chain. As on the camshaft bearing housings the starter motor covers had an '860' engraving. Other 860GTS engine updates included new inlet and exhaust valves and new valve guides. The cylinder heads also carried different part numbers, and the carburettors featured new banjo connections and idle screws. The carburettor air filtration was improved for the GTS, with the pleated soft hoses changing to a harder plastic. Although the Lafranconi mufflers were unchanged, the 860 GTS exhaust header pipes were dual walled to reduce exhaust bluing.

Chassis

The 860 GTS frame number sequence and DGM homologation number was the same as that of the 860 GT, and the frame was identical but for the rear subframe. Also similar was the suspension, including a 38mm Ceriani front fork and 320mm Marzocchi shock absorbers. The front fork had the usual Ceriani black triple clamps and polished fork legs, but with 750-style chromed headlight supports (without rubber bushes). The Marzocchi shock absorbers still featured chrome springs and black plastic covers, but the spring preload was now adjustable for five positions (instead of three).

Although the Radaelli 18in wheels and 200mm rear drum brake were unchanged from the 860 GT, all 860 GTSs came with a dual 280mm disc

34

The Marzocchi shock absorbers on the 860 GTS now featured five spring preload positions.

Brembo front brake. The front master cylinder with solid reservoir was unchanged, but now included the eccentric adjuster at the lever. The Brembo 08 brake calipers still incorporated twin bleed valves, 'BREMBO' insignia, and plastic pad covers. The tyres were Metzeler or Pirelli, mostly Metzeler, a 3.50H18 C66 on the front and a 4.00 or 120/90H18 C88 on the rear.

The 860 GTS's raison d'être was to provide a more European and sporting image so most of the updates were cosmetic. These concentrated on the rounder 18-litre fuel tank and lower seat, extending to lower handlebars and a more functional instrument layout. The fuel tank still featured Brev Orlandi fuel taps with green plastic fuel lines. As on the 860 GT, the GTS seat hinged on the left, and was lockable, now with a Neiman lock similar to that on the steering head (but still with a different key). There was an aluminium strip on each side of the seat, and a strap. The first 860 GTSs used decals (not badges) on the fuel tank and side covers, and there was a yellow 'Made in Italy' decal below the filler cap. Not long after production was implemented, the fuel tank 'DUCATI' and side cover '860' decals were changed to badges. The 'GTS' remained a decal. The side covers were unchanged from the 860 GT, as were the painted steel front and rear mudguards, but with mudguard decals matching those of the fuel tank. The range of colours was fewer for the GTS, with 1976 examples either orange with black stripes, or metallic blue with silver stripes. The stripes on the mudguards were narrower than on the 860 GT. Red, black, yellow, and green bodywork wasn't available on the GTS for 1976, but some of these colours became available in 1977. There was now a chrome-plated lifting handle on the left-hand side to help place the machine on the centre stand. Early GTSs didn't have a side stand.

Along with the updated fuel tank and seat, the most noticeable difference was the instrument panel. The two Smiths instruments were mounted in the rubber pods of the 750 Sport, held in place with the same metal straps with a swivelling screw. The speedometer was still mounted on the left and the tachometer on the right, and UK versions received a 150mph speedometer.

Polished aluminium U-bolts no longer

The 860 GTS fuel tank was rounder than that of the 860 GT, and the seat new. Wiring still included an Aprilia fuse box. (Courtesy Two Wheels)

Although the 860 GTS retained Smiths instruments, they were mounted individually, with a new warning light display.

860 GTS was still the same square CEV as the 860 GT, but a Bosch starter relay solved the problem of burnt out starting switches. This starter relay was situated under the left side cover, next to the air cleaner. The wiring loom was also new, the ignition now feeding into the main loom rather than through the headlight.

The lower and flatter handlebar was similar to that of the European specification 750 GT, and some of the very earliest models included the choke on the handlebar. After only a few examples the choke moved from the clutch perch to a white plastic lever attached to the instrument support. These 860 GTSs used a new clutch lever bracket, but all featured the rubber Verlicchi handgrips. 1976 860 GTSs also came with an Aprilia JOD Duplo 55/60W halogen headlamp with black shell, 3W parking light, and 5/21W CEV taillight. The Aprilia indicators were the rounded 21W type.

Although the 860 GTS was a brave attempt by Ducati to revive the unsuccessful 860 GT, it wasn't as popular as originally envisaged. Due to a large stockpile of unsold 860 GTs and parallel twins, motorcycle production slumped to 4053 in 1976. Only 510 860 GTSs were built this year, and more than a quarter of motorcycle production was the 125cc Scramblers. During 1976 there was a possibility that Ducati Meccanica would cease to exist as a motorcycle manufacturer, but the success of the 900 Super Sport provided a reprieve.

clamped the narrower and lower handlebar to the top triple clamp, as this was incorporated with the Aprilia dashboard. This also included five small warning lights, the city/country horn switch, and the six-pin ignition switch. To prevent water entering the switch while at rest there was a rubber cover for the ignition switch. Unlike the 860 GT, the GTS warning lights were smaller LED lamps. These were for lights (green), high beam (red), generator (red), neutral (yellow), and indicators (yellow). The single two-volume Belli horn of the 860 GT was retained. The switchgear on the early

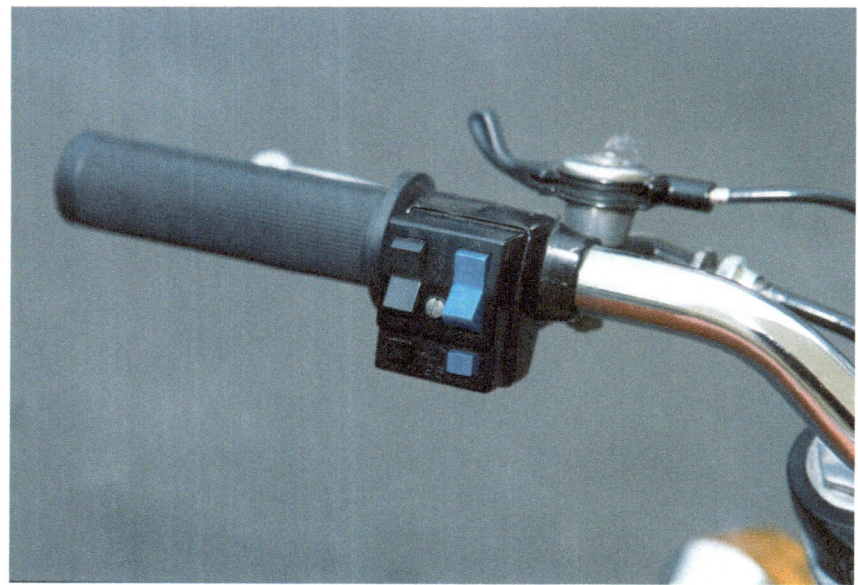

Some of the earliest 860 GTS had the choke lever on the handlebar, as on the 860 GT.

The 860 GTS taillight was CEV, and the indicators Aprilia.

There was some inconsistency in the exact specification of examples displayed at motorcycle shows. This 860 GTS has different decals, 860 GT side cover badges, rectangular turn signals, and a choke lever near the instruments. (Courtesy Two Wheels)

Most 1976 860 GTSs were like this, with fuel tank and side cover decals. (Courtesy Two Wheels)

1976 860 GTS distinguishing features (from engine number approx. DM860 852000-853788, frame number approx. DM860S 853000-853669)

Engine
Seeger ring location for right-side shifting lever
New gearbox layshaft and 5th gear
36-tooth kick-start shaft gear
Different clutch to 860 GT with 750 inner clutch drum and new clutch housing
After engine number 852177 another new clutch drum with new bearings
New electric start motor and gearing with 15-tooth sprocket and 40-link chain
New inlet and exhaust valves and new valve guides
New cylinder heads
New carburettor banjo connections and idle screws
Hard plastic air filter hoses
Lafranconi mufflers and dual walled exhaust header pipes

Chassis
New frame but with DM860S and DGM 13715 OM homologation number
38mm Ceriani front fork with polished alloy fork legs and black triple clamps

280mm Brembo 08 front disc front brake
Front master cylinder without eccentric lever adjustment
750 GT-style chromed headlight supports
320mm Marzocchi rear shock absorbers with five preload positions, black spring covers, and chrome-plated springs
18in steel-rimmed Radaelli wheels front and rear
Smiths instruments located in rubber pods
Dashboard with handlebar clamp and five LED warning lights
City/country horn
Narrower and lower handlebar
Alloy choke lever on left handlebar on early examples
CEV handlebar switches (as on 860 GT)
Aprilia turn signals
Aprilia 170mm JOD Duplo H4 headlight
CEV taillight
Rounder 18-litre steel fuel tank (early examples with tank decals and not badges)
Lower seat
Painted steel mudguards
Chrome-plated lifting handle on the left

CHAPTER FOUR

1977 – 750 AND 900 SUPER SPORT, 860/900 GTS, 900 SPORT 'DARMAH'

Ducati was in crisis by mid-1976. The failure of the company's new models (125 Regolarità, 860, and 350/500 GTL) saw the EFIM Group consider merging Ducati with MV Agusta. EFIM bought 51 per cent of MV Agusta in 1974, but the companies were always separate within the organisation. This merger didn't eventuate, and a new director, Ing. Sebastiano Leonardi replaced Zauibouri. Leonardi was committed to increasing motorcycle production but wanted to concentrate on smaller capacity models. Along with the 125 Six Days and 500 GTV, he had Taglioni design a belt-drive overhead camshaft single, and authorized a new generation bevel-drive twin, the 900 Sport Darmah. From September 1976 bevel-drive twin production centred on the new Super Sport, and during 1977 the production 900 Sport Desmo was introduced. Both these models were successful and motorcycle production approached the levels of the halcyon days of 1973 and 1974. 7167 machines left the production line at Borgo Panigale during 1977, 3043 of these bevel-drive twins.

750 and 900 Super Sport

Regular Super Sport production was approved early in 1976, with the proviso that the SS meet registration requirements in all countries. This stipulation saw a steel fuel tank for the UK, left-side gearshift for the US, and reduced noise in general through the use of a quieter intake and exhaust system. The updated Super Sport also continued Ducati's dubious tradition of gradually downgrading the specification of models as time progressed. This was evident with the evolution of the 750 GT and Sport between 1971 and 1974, these models ultimately incorporating a variety of budget components. The same happened to the Super Sport during 1976. However, while some of the purity of the original was lost, the soul was, fortunately, kept intact, the Super Sport continuing Ducati's fine tradition of building supreme sporting motorcycles. Although an owner's manual was printed in February 1976 that did include some information on a 1976 model (without pictures) it wasn't until July that a prototype 900 Super Sport was sent to Australia to gauge reaction as a prelude to a production version. While featuring

The prototype 1977 900 Super Sport was built during 1976. The frame was painted blue and the seat and kick-start lever were from the 1975 Super Sport. (Courtesy Two Wheels)

the steel fuel tank and Lafranconi mufflers, this example had a blue-painted frame, a 1975 kick-start lever, and 1975 shock absorbers. This prototype also had an ill-fitting 1975 seat (without rubber seal) that didn't match the hastily modified 750 Sport steel fuel tank. The footpegs were also specially-fabricated and the instruments Smiths, but many of the updated features appeared on this prototype. These included the new Aprilia handlebar switches, steel fuel tank, Lafranconi mufflers, left-side gear shift, and right-side rear brake setup. Unlike the eventual production version this prototype also had a standard 860 clutch cover and crossover shaft, with specially-fabricated gear and brake linkages.

Production of the new Super Sport commenced during September 1976 and, by the end of the year 1020 900 Super Sports were built. This included 520 for Europe and the rest of the world as homologation models, 280 as non-homologation, and 220 for the US as homologation. The homologation versions featured quieter mufflers and smaller carburettors, while the non-homologation examples were identical, but included the earlier 40mm carburettors and Conti mufflers as a performance kit. There were also 220 similar 750 Super Sports produced during this period, 120 as non-homologation examples for production racing in Italy. Although Ducati lists the first examples of these Super Sports as 1976 models, as they were built after September 1976 and were generally not available until 1977,

it's easier to consider them 1977 versions. The owner's manual that specifically covered this model was published in February 1977. Super Sport production continued into 1977, but on a reduced scale as development now concentrated on the Darmah. 496 were produced for Europe, all as homologation examples, plus 137 for the US. 100 750 Super Sports were built in 1977, all as homologation examples.

Engine

The engine specifications were essentially unchanged from 1975, with the engine number sequence for both the 750 and 900 Super Sports continuing where the 1975 series finished. 1977 900 Super Sports began at engine number 086251, with the 750 beginning at 075662. Initially all these still featured the '.1' designation, but at some stage during early 1977 this disappeared from the crankcases on the 900, although it still remained on the 750. Instead of the '.1' some 900 engines included a stamped 'D' after the DM860. The first 1977 Super Sports also featured polished valve rockers, but during 1977 these became regular forged items. As the 1975 versions, the 750 engine was visually identical, and still a sleeved-down 860, but for the '750' camshaft bearing housings. The 900 bearing housings were as before, without '860' insignia.

Inside the Super Sport engine there were

The 900 Super Sport engine was unchanged for 1977, but the Lafranconi mufflers hurt performance. (Courtesy Two Wheels)

Dell'Orto 32mm carburettors with air cleaners were standard, and the rear brake moved to the right for 1977. The kick-start lever and gearshift were new. (Courtesy Two Wheels)

only a few updates for 1977. The clutch housing and inner clutch drum were again changed, with the housing now featuring two different bearings, (25x47x12mm and 25x52x15mm). This was similar to the earlier 1973-74 Super Sport, but the inner clutch drum was longer and the clutch consisted of eight steel driving plates and eight fibre driven plates. While the Ducati Elettrotecnica ignition system was unchanged the spark plugs were Champion L82Y and the maximum ignition advance was slightly reduced. Maximum advance was specified at 32-34 degrees for the 900 and 34-36 degrees for the 750.

Starting remained at kick only but new for 1977 was a 36-tooth kick-start gear to improve the start ratio. There was also a new kick-start lever, designed to clear the revised footpeg. The most major update was the incorporation of the crossover gearshift system of the 860 GT to provide left-side shifting. As on the 860, the selector mechanism was still housed in the right rear engine cover. The crossover shaft was slightly shorter than that used on the 860, and the outer clutch cover was different.

Although the Dell'Orto PHM 40A carburettors were fitted to non-homologated 900 Super Sports (but with aluminium rather than welded steel intake manifolds) the standard equipment for the 1977

Super Sport was a pair of Dell'Orto PHF 32A carburettors. These came with air cleaners and cable-operated chokes. The white plastic choke lever was mounted on a bracket on the left rear downtube, behind the fuel tank, and controlled

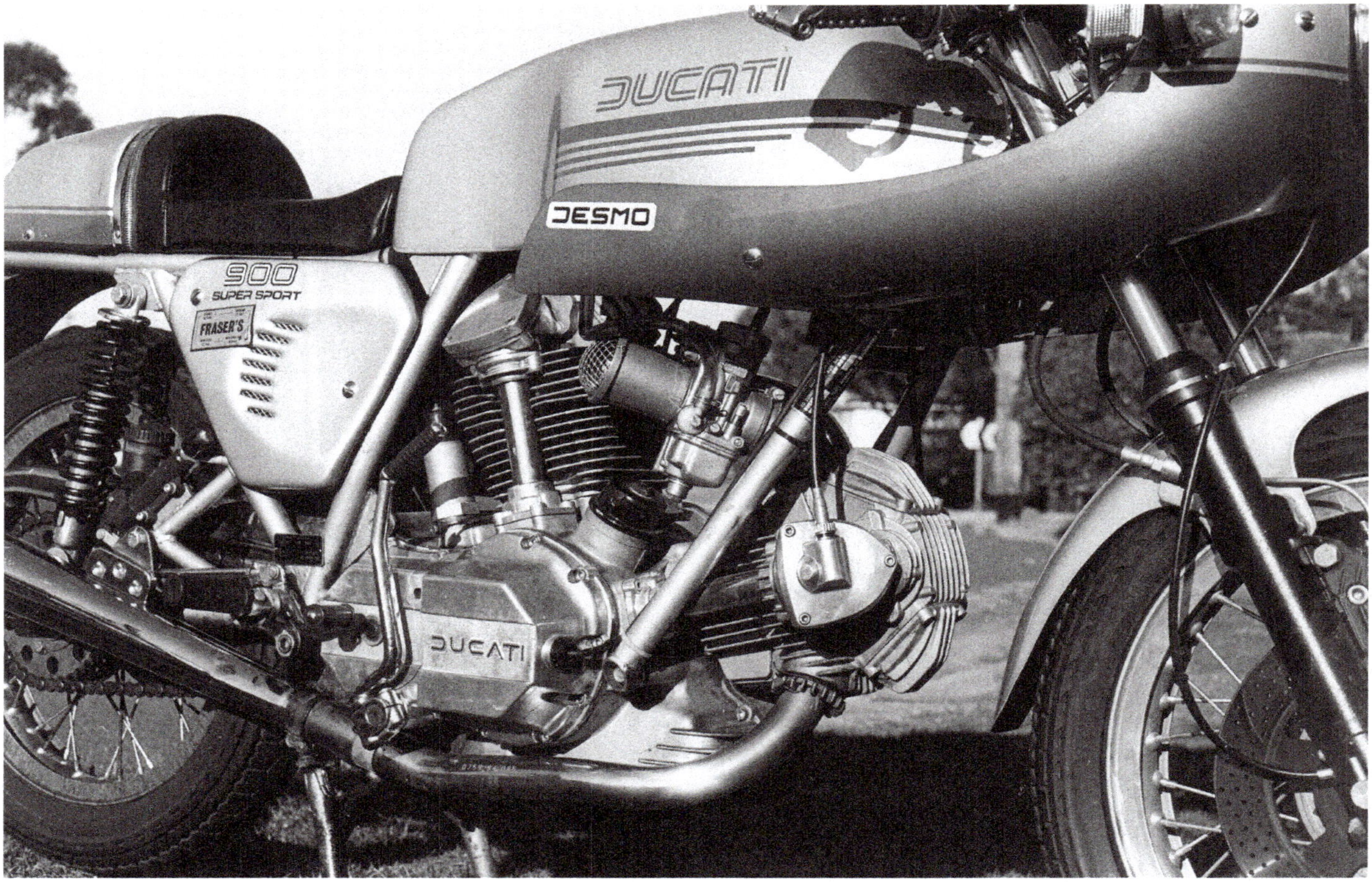

Dell'Orto 40mm carburettors and Conti mufflers were an option for the 1977 Super Sport. The Contis now had a larger bracket. The brake disc drilling pattern was also different this year. (Courtesy Two Wheels*)*

the chokes through two cables. Initially the carburettors featured metal banjo fuel line unions, these soon becoming white plastic, without a sealing washer. The idle speed screw was also changed during early production, and a gasket installed behind the accelerator pump diaphragm. The aluminium float bowls were no longer polished, but the float bowl was still retained by a 14mm hex nut. All 40mm carburettors were the newer type with provision for a choke attachment.

Silver-painted steel air boxes were mounted on the frame under the fuel tank, and behind the left-side cover, and contained pleated paper filters. The air intakes were 860 GTS-style hard plastic, and the versions with 40mm carburettors featured the usual open bell mouths with wire mesh filters. On the 1977 Super Sport

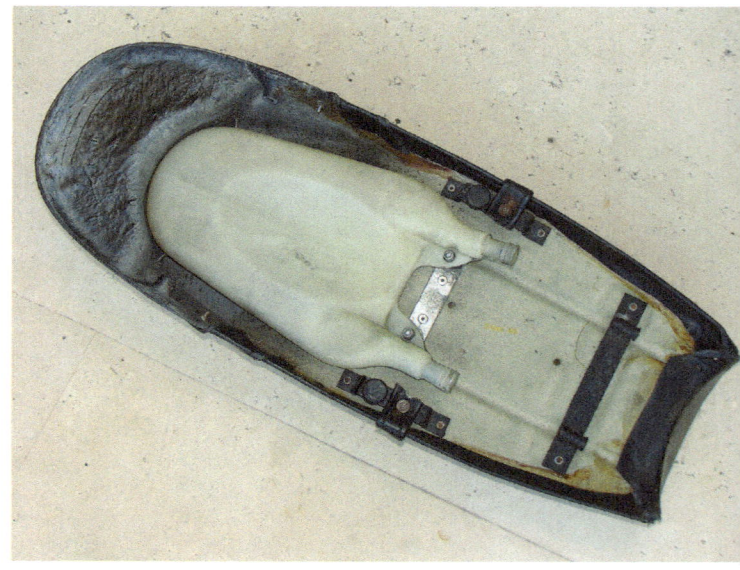

For 1977 the engine breather chamber was incorporated under the seat. This is a later dual seat but the solo seat arrangement was similar. (Courtesy Nico Georgeoglou)

the mesh was wire as on the 1975 examples. The engine breather was also quite different for 1976, no longer venting through a flapper valve into the atmosphere. Underneath the fibreglass solo seat was a plastic engine breather chamber connected to the breather labyrinth.

The homologated exhaust system was also new for 1976. This comprised new header pipes, exhaust clamps, and Lafranconi mufflers. The Lafranconis were the same as for the 860, without a kick-start recess on the right. Conti mufflers were still available as an option, but with a larger bracket. The clamps were also different to earlier versions, with 'Conti' lettering and with hex bolts instead of special Allen bolts. To provide more clearance for the shock absorber mounts a 11.5x20x10mm spacer fitted between the muffler and the frame mount, requiring a longer muffler bolt (7⁄16in x32mm).

Chassis

While the basic dimensions of the silver-painted frame were unchanged for 1976, there was a new series of frame numbers and new frame homologation number for the 900 (DGM 13715 OM). Frame numbers now carried a DM860SS prefix, beginning at 086001. The 750 Super Sport frame carried on with the earlier DM750SS number sequence (from 075912) and DGM 11871 OM homologation number. All Super Sports this year also received a new silencer homologation number, E3-9R-13716, the plate now positioned underneath the right side cover because the previous location on the frame was cut away for the left-side gearshift. The main changes to the frame were to the brackets for mounting the air filter boxes, regulator, fuel tank, ignition transducers, and the angle of the rear muffler mounting bracket to incorporate the right-side rear brake and master cylinder. To allow for the air filter underneath the left side cover, the regulator was moved to the right, on the rear frame tube next to the battery. The tank mounting bracket also included provision for fitting an optional fibreglass 'Imola' tank.

Although the colour scheme, fibreglass mudguards, and side covers remained as before, there were changes to the fuel tank and fairing for 1976. With fibreglass fuel tanks now illegal in

Only a small number of 750 Super Sports were built for 1977, still with the silver and blue fairing. (Courtesy Ducati Motor)

The frame for 1977 now carried a DM860SS designation, and included a differently-angled muffler bracket. The gearshift was now on the left, and a choke lever was mounted on the left. The previous ignition key hole was now filled.

many markets the distinctive 'Imola'-style tank made way for an 18-litre steel tank. This was identical in shape to the tank on the 1974 750 Sport, with the filler tap opening away from the rider, but with two frame mounted rubber buffers to isolate the tank from vibration. The fuel taps were unchanged, although the stamp was now Paioli instead of Brev Orlandi, following a Paioli purchase of Orlandi. Because the steel tank was narrower than the fibreglass type it also required revised mounting brackets on the frame. The decals were new, and the Giugiaro 'DUCATI' lettering was blue instead of black and white. The side cover decals were as before, as were the 'DESMO' fairing and seat decals.

The fairing was reshaped (slightly taller, narrower, and with a taller screen) and now incorporated cut-outs for the installation of direction indicators. There were also new fairing mounts (with the front screws closer together) and initially the fairing screen was plain Plexiglas and the seven slotted retaining screws were as for 1975. During 1977 the screen featured a protective beading and the screws changed to the US specification type with locating cups. As well as incorporating the breather chamber, the solo seat was also longer to join the shorter steel fuel tank. The seat padding kicked up at the front. During 1977 a dual seat became available, although this wasn't initially fitted as standard equipment.

Along with the engine breather chamber this seat featured a small, rear opening, lockable compartment.

While the Marzocchi front fork was unchanged, the rear five-position 310mm shock absorbers were new. Still with black springs, these no longer featured the black rubber covers over the top of the spring and during 1977 included small red 'Marzocchi' decals. The Borrani 4777 18in alloy wheel rims were also unchanged, but differed in that the rims were straight in section and not flared. Super Sports built in 1976 and 1977 were also fitted with different tyres, Pirelli Gordon Super Sport MT 18 (3.50V18 and 120/90V18) for those machines built in 1976, and Michelin M45 (3.50V18 and 4.25/85V18) for 1977. The final drive gearing was changed from 1975, with the 900 generally having a 15-tooth front sprocket, and a 36-tooth rear sprocket. The 750 Super Sport had a 38-tooth rear sprocket, as did US examples of the 900 Super Sport. Accompanying the smaller sprockets was a shorter (102-link) Renold BS $\frac{5}{8}$x$\frac{3}{8}$in chain.

But for modifications to allow for the rear brake to operate from the right, the Brembo triple disc braking system was essentially unchanged from 1975. The rear master cylinder was positioned on the right muffler frame bracket and this new type included a clear reservoir. The brake light pressure switch was on the master cylinder. The

Apart from the reshaped rim, the rear wheel and disc brake were unchanged from 1975. (Courtesy Two Wheels)

front brake master cylinder was initially the 1975 solid reservoir type, but with a mirror mount. During 1977 there was a new front master cylinder, sitting closer to the handlebar, with a clear plastic fluid reservoir and also a mirror mount. A new black lever now included a recessed Allen screw and eccentric adjuster. The 280mm drilled front discs also featured a slightly different pattern, with rows of eight holes instead of seven.

There were new chrome-plated clip-on handlebars for the 1977 Super Sport, these featuring 6x35mm hexagon retaining bolts rather than Allen screws. Instead of two holes drilled in the left handlebar for the chrome-plated Aprilia switch, the left handlebar was serrated for the updated Aprilia switch. The black clutch lever was also new, now shaped to match the angular brake lever, but the clutch perch was unchanged and still without a mirror mount. During 1977 the clutch perch changed to include a mirror mount. Initially the rubber Verlicchi handgrips were the same as before but were changed during 1977 to a Verlicchi with a revised pattern.

One of the most significant updates for the 1977 Super Sport was the altered riding position due to repositioned footpegs. Instead of lugs welded to the frame the slightly rear-set footpegs were mounted on the serrations near the swingarm pivot. The footpegs were rubber, and the chrome-plated steel gearshift and brake levers were mounted on screws into these brackets. The

footpeg and lever setup for this series of Super Sport was hastily conceived and was an inferior solution that was later rectified. To enable the Super Sport to be street legal in most countries Aprilia direction indicators were also fitted. Mounted on chrome-plated steel brackets, the indicators varied slightly for different markets and from bike-to-bike. Some were chrome without side reflectors, while others were black, with or without side reflectors.

Although the Ducati Elettrotecnica ignition was unchanged from 1975, for the 1977 Super Sport was a new Aprilia wiring loom similar to that of the 860 GTS. This included a series of multi-plug connectors, but retained the previous fusebox. The engine stop relay was now inside

The first series of 1977 Super Sport featured a three-light dashboard, with the same markings as for 1975. (Courtesy Tony Hennagan)

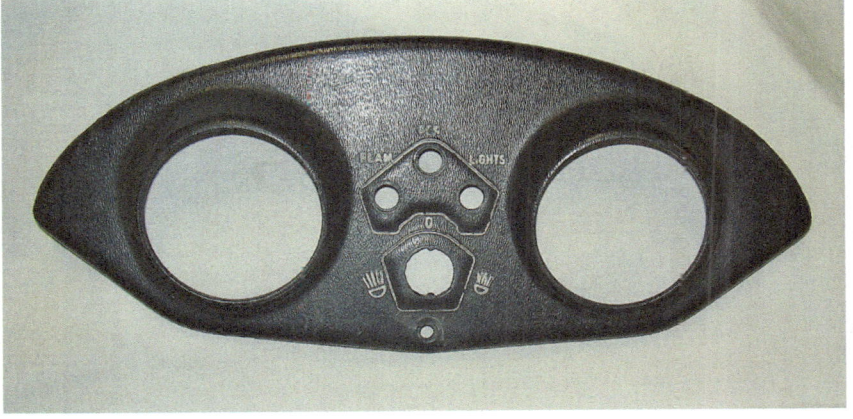

The first type of three-light dashboard was soon replaced by this dash, with P and R markings. The Veglia speedometer didn't include a trip meter, and the tachometer redline was 8000rpm.

The earliest examples of the 1977 900 Super Sport had this Aprilia handlebar switch modelled on the Japanese ND type.

the headlamp shell, and the regulator moved under the right side cover, behind the battery. The earliest 1977 examples featured a new Aprilia left handlebar switch (36387 AE QB 3) that controlled the lights, high and low beam, headlamp flasher and right and left indicators. The chrome-plated Tommaselli Daytona 2C throttle control featured a revised location for the throttle stop screw, now underneath instead of on top. There was also a new Aprilia black plastic instrument panel, similar to the 1975 version but incorporating the ignition switch instead of the earlier light switch. There were three warning lights (Beam, Gen, and Lights), in a triangle with a thin white line accentuating them. Despite the light switch being moved to the handlebar there were still the light indications on either side of the ignition key. Two types of three-light dash were fitted, one with light indications (as on the 1975 dash) and another later type with P (Park), O (Off), and R (Run). On both types there was a round hole for the six-pin, three-position ignition key. Both types of three-light Aprilia instrument panels differed for the US examples but during 1977 all Super Sports were standardized with a five-light CEV dashboard and CEV handlebar switches.

Initially the 1977 Super Sport retained the earlier Smiths instruments (for Europe and the US) but during 1977 some European specification Super Sports were fitted with Veglia Borletti instruments. These were similar to those of the final 750 Sport, but were mounted with the speedometer on the right and tachometer on the left. The tachometer featured an 8000rpm redline, and

the speedometer was now without a trip meter. While the Aprilia headlamp, small CEV taillight, and single Belli horn were unchanged, the headlamp shell was now black.

With production levels increased substantially over the 1975 version, the 1977 Super Sport re-established Ducati as a premier manufacturer of sporting motorcycles. Still with a frame designed in 1971, even in 1977 the Super Sport set the sporting standard for handling and braking. With the optional 40mm carburettors and Conti mufflers the engine performance rivalled that of any comparable machine. The success of the 750 and 900 Super Sport during 1977 was fundamental in the decision by the EFIM to continue producing motorcycles.

US specification 900 Super Sport 1977

A significant proportion of model year 1977 900 Super Sport production (220 in 1976 and 137 in 1977) was intended for the US, and these machines included some differences to European versions. While the engine and frame specifications were unchanged, the wiring and some electrical equipment was different. All US Super Sports came with 32mm carburettors and Lafranconi mufflers as standard equipment and shared the engine and frame number sequence with European versions. Some early frames were also without the DGM frame homologation number stamp.

US 900 Super Sports had an updated wiring system. This included a new wiring loom with four multi-pin connectors, and an Aprilia fusebox with three fuses (two 8A and one 25A). There was an Aprilia sealed beam headlamp, without a parking light, and a black headlamp shell. The flash relay was positioned near the fusebox with the engine stop relay incorporated as part of the wiring loom, and connected to a chrome-plated CEV engine stop switch on the right handlebar.

Other changes specific to the US Super Sport included a CEV left-side switch block (instead of Aprilia). There was also a revised Aprilia instrument panel, with five warning lights. Joining the earlier three was a yellow indicator light and a green neutral light. The ignition key was a four-pin type, and still three-position. Only Smiths instruments (a 150mph speedometer) appear to have been fitted to the 1977 US Super Sports, but the five-light dashboard and CEV switches soon featured on European specification Super Sports.

The Brembo front brake master cylinder was generally the later type (with a clear fluid reservoir)

US Super Sports had an engine stop switch on the right handlebar.

The left-side switch was CEV instead of Aprilia on the US Super Sport

US Super Sports in 1977 also had a five-light Aprilia dashboard.

and there was a new fairing for the US Super Sport. This featured a larger opening for the headlamp (sealed by a longer 700mm gasket), and a different frame-mounted support bracket. The front fairing brackets were also different, with the two holes on each side closer together. There were also new CEV indicators (with side reflectors) and different brackets. Most US fairings had a plexiglass screen

Racing the 1977 Super Sport

In March 1977 Greg Johnson rode a 1977 model 900 Super Sport to victory in the Adelaide Three-hour production race. Fitted with the optional 20-litre fibreglass fuel tank, Johnson won ahead of Kenny Blake and Mick Cole on a 1975 900 Super Sport. During 1977 the 900 Super Sport was gradually outclassed in open production racing but the 750 SS remained competitive. Mike Hailwood teamed with Jim Scaysbrook on a 1977 model 750 Super Sport for the 1977 Castrol Six-hour race, the pair finishing sixth overall and second in the 750 class. Roy Denison and Geoff Sim also rode a 750 Super Sport to a 750 class victory in the 1978 Surfers Three-hour race. Hailwood rode the 750 Super Sport again in the 1978 Castrol Six-hour race but this time retired after Scaysbrook crashed while leading the 750 class.

The front fairing screws were closer together on the US Super Sport.

1977 750 Super Sport distinguishing features (from engine number DM750.1 075662-075982 approx., frame numbers DM750SS 075912-076225 approx.)

1977 900 Super Sport distinguishing features (from engine number DM860.1 086251-087600 approx.; frame number DM860SS 086001-087500 approx.)

Engine

Initially crankcases featured the ".1" designation.

During 1977 900 becomes DM860, sometimes with a "D".

Early 1977 Super Sports featured polished valve rockers

New clutch housing and inner clutch drum

Champion L82Y spark plugs

Maximum advance 32-34 degrees for the 900 and 34-36 degrees for the 750

36-tooth kick start gear and new kick start lever

Left side gear shift with the selector mechanism on the right and shorter crossover shaft than the 860

Different clutch cover

Dell'Orto PHM 40A of PHF 32A carburettors with aluminium intake manifolds. 32mm carburettors with air cleaners and cable operated chokes operated by a white plastic lever mounted on a bracket behind the fuel tank.

Carburettors initially featured metal banjo fuel line unions but most were white plastic

During 1977 the idle speed screw changed, and a gasket installed behind the accelerator pump diaphragm.

Carburettor float bowls no longer polished

40mm carburettors with provision for a choke attachment and wire mesh bell mouths

Silver painted steel air boxes for 32mm carburettors

Engine breather chamber incorporated in the fibreglass solo seat base

New homologated exhaust system with new header pipes, exhaust clamps, and Lafranconi mufflers (right side without kick-start recess)

Conti mufflers still available as an option, but with a larger bracket

Chassis

New frame number sequence for 900 SS beginning at DM860SS 086001

New frame homologation number for the 900 SS (DGM 13715 OM)

New silencer homologation number E3-9R-13716

New brackets for air filter boxes, regulator, fuel tank, and revised angle of the rear muffler mounting bracket

Regulator moved to the right

18-litre steel fuel tank with Paioli fuel taps

New fairing, with cut-outs for indicators, and new fairing mounts

Later screens with protective beading

Seat longer, with kicked up padding and plastic breather chamber

Dual seat available during 1977

New Marzocchi five-position 310mm shock absorbers without top rubber covers

Borrani 4777 18-inch alloy wheel rims with straight section rims

Eight hole spiral pattern drilled front brake discs

Rear brake master cylinder moved to the right muffler frame bracket

Rear brake light switch on the master cylinder

Front brake master cylinder was initially the solid reservoir type, with a mirror mount

New front master cylinder during 1977, sitting closer to the handlebar, with a clear plastic fluid reservoir

Clip-on handlebars featured 6x35mm hexagon retaining bolts

Black clutch lever shaped to match the angular brake lever

Clutch perch initially without a mirror mount

Verlicchi handgrips as before but with a new pattern during 1977

Repositioned rubber footpegs for right side brake and left-side gear shift

Aprilia direction indicators, some chrome without side reflectors and others black, with or without side reflectors

New wiring loom and Aprilia handlebar switch

Different wiring for most US versions

CEV handlebar switch for the US and standardised during 1977

US versions with CEV engine stop button on right handlebar

Engine stop relay was inside the black headlamp shell

Tommaselli Daytona 2C throttle with throttle stop screw underneath

Two types of three-light Aprilia instrument panel incorporating the ignition switch

US five-light instrument panel standardised during 1977

Initially with Smiths instruments

Most with Veglia instruments (with 8,000rpm redline tachometer and no trip meter speedometer)

with a protective beading, the screen retained by seven 4x15mm screws with additional cups. There was also a different rear mudguard incorporating a metal reinforcing plate to support the larger CEV taillight and bracket.

860/900 GTS

By 1977 there were still stocks of unsold kick-start 860 GTs and, as had happened in 1976, many were fitted with an 860 GTS fuel tank and lower seat. These were sold at bargain prices under various designations (860 GTL or 860 Mk III) while the 860 GTS continued with a few updates. It is convenient to consider the 1977 860 GTS beginning after engine number 853787 and frame number 853669 when most of these updates occurred. Towards the end of 1977 production the designation also changed from 860 to 900 GTS.

Engine

While the basic engine was as before, there were a few modifications after engine number 853787. An inner valve spring was added to the existing single valve springs, and there were new camshafts, with revised timing. Along with the camshafts were new valves and guides, and valve guide seals, while the exhaust header pipes were now dual wall to reduce the problem of bluing. The rectangular camshaft bearing housings were also the 900 SS type, without 860 inscriptions, and the 30mm lock ring attaching the stator ignition cables to the left crankcase was modified, now requiring a special tool for removal. From engine number 853918 the bearing support plate for the camshaft drive was updated, with new bearings.

Chassis

After frame number 853669 a Marzocchi front fork replaced the Ceriani. The Marzocchi included 38x600mm fork tubes and offset triple clamps to provide slightly less trail and lighter steering. As with the Cerianis the fork legs were polished aluminium, with black triple clamps, but the Marzocchi fork included a different Brembo brake caliper mount (identical to the Super Sport). The thread was now incorporated in the fork slider rather than the brake caliper. Initially, the front master cylinder was the 1976 type, without a clear

reservoir, but was soon changed to the later type (with clear reservoir). The Radaelli wheels and 320mm Marzocchi shock absorbers with black covers and chrome springs were unchanged, while the swingarm now featured a grease nipple instead of the 6mm oil nipple. For 1977 there was a noticeable improvement in the finish. With the Marzocchi fork, more durable 'Inox' stainless steel mudguards replaced the painted steel type, and the paint was improved. Metal badges replaced the decals on the fuel tank and side covers, although the '860' side cover badges still included a 'GTS' decal. When the designation changed to 900 GTS the side covers had '900' decals.

There were a number of updates to the electrical specification. As the 860 GTS was now produced as a US version there was a new wiring loom with updated connectors. The relays were still located inside the black Aprilia headlight shell, with the same JOD Duplo halogen headlight (or sealed beam for the US). Initially, the instrument panel (including the city/country horn), square 860 GT-style CEV switch blocks, clutch cable adjustment, and throttle remained as for the 1976 860 GTS. While most 860 GTSs were also fitted with Smiths instruments, some also left the factory with Veglia instruments. Some of the Smiths tachometers were also the earlier type (as fitted to the 1971 750 GT) with a 10,000rpm redline.

Early in 1977 the European 860 GTS was updated with new CEV electrical equipment. This included a CEV instrument panel, without the town/country horn switch, a new four-position ignition key, and five LED warning lights. There were also new CEV handlebar switches with external wiring, CEV indicators, and a CEV headlight with a chrome-plated shell. The 860 GTS also received a new handlebar, clutch cable and adjusters, clutch lever and support. While the clutch lever bracket was black, both the clutch and brake levers were

For 1977 the 860 GTS received a Marzocchi front fork and stainless steel mudguards (Courtesy Ducati Victor)

860 GTS wheel rims were always Radaelli Ramon Sport. (Courtesy Nico Georgeoglou)

polished aluminium. The clutch adjuster with rubber cover was the same as on the 750/900 Super Sport. The horn was initially still a single Voxbell, and the new wiring included a small Bosch three-fuse fusebox (two 8A and one 25A). The relays were no longer inside the headlight shell, the Bosch electric start relay now mounted on the centre frame tube under the tank. The turn signal relay hung loose under the seat on a small rubber. The throttle assembly was a black Tommaselli and CEV combination that included the electric start and engine stop switch. This part was specific to the 860/900 GTS as it was the only electric start bevel-twin with CEV switches. The hand grips

Another view of the 1977 860 GTS. Badges replaced the tank and side cover decals this year. (Courtesy Two Wheels)

1977 860/900 GTS distinguishing features (from engine number DM860 853789-854250 approx., frame number DM860S 853670-854200 approx.)

Engine
An inner valve spring was added to the existing single valve springs
New camshafts with revised timing
New valves and valve guides
New valve guide seals
Dual wall exhaust header pipes
Camshaft bearing housings 900 SS type
New ignition stator cable 30mm lock ring
From engine number 853918 new camshaft drive bearing support plate

Chassis
Marzocchi front fork with polished aluminium fork legs and black triple clamps
New Brembo front brake calipers with different mount
Grease nipple in swingarm instead of the 6mm oil nipple

'Inox' stainless steel mudguards
Badges on the fuel tank and side covers
New wiring loom with updated connectors
Relays still located inside the black Aprilia headlight shell with JOD Duplo headlight
Initially with the same Aprilia instrument panel (including city/country horn)
Initially with square CEV switches and throttle
Most with Smiths instruments but some with Veglia
During 1977 CEV switches, indicators, instrument panel and headlight fitted with new wiring, fusebox, and relays
US versions retained Aprilia indicators
860 GTS became 900 GTS during 1977 with '900 GTS' side cover decals

were the harder rubber Verlicchi. US examples retained the Aprilia headlight and indicators, but included the new wiring loom with small fusebox and relays. All 1977 860/900 GTSs were built in the early part of 1977 as the bevel production line was preparing for the new Darmah.

900 Sport Desmo 'Darmah'

A change swept through motorcycling during 1976. Styling and fashion took precedence and dictated new features, while the market demanded a greater degree of refinement and improved ergonomics. Ducati responded with the 900 Sport Darmah, the most radical incarnation of the bevel-drive twin yet. Instead of producing what it believed the market wanted (such as the 860 and parallel twin), Ducati now took a pragmatic approach. The 900 SD was the first Ducati to feature Japanese instruments and switches, German ignition, cast alloy wheels, and an hydraulic steering damper.

As with the 860, Ducati decided to outsource the styling, this time entrusting the design to Leopoldo Tartarini of nearby Italjet. Tartarini had a long association with Ducati and, although he was responsible for the 1975 Indian 860 fiasco this didn't seem to hurt his relationship with Ducati. Tartarini was responsible for some of the better Ducati designs of the early 1970s (1973 750 Sport and Desmo singles) and this obviously stood him in good stead. The prototype 900 Sport 'Darmah' was displayed at the Bologna show at the end of 1976. It was heavily based around an 860 GTS but with silver-painted, cast aluminium FPS 18in wheels (similar to those of the Moto Guzzi 850 Le Mans), triple 280mm Brembo disc brakes, Nippon Denso instruments and switchgear, and a small clear plastic handlebar-mounted screen. The engine in the prototype was still based on the 860 GTS, with a crossover left side gearshift and Ducati Elettrotecnica ignition. The bike had the designation 'Darmah', after the name of a tiger in an Italian children's story. When the 900

SD went into production in July 1977 its final form was considerably different to the prototype. In ancillary and electrical equipment the 900 SD was a huge step forward for Ducati, and few parts were shared with the earlier 860s. By August 1977 the first examples appeared in Italy and the UK so the early 900 SD can be considered a 1977 model.

Engine

Ducati was encouraged by the success of the desmodromic Super Sport in 1975 and Taglioni persuaded Ducati's directors to produce the next generation 900 Ducati with desmodromic valve gear. He already envisaged the entire Ducati

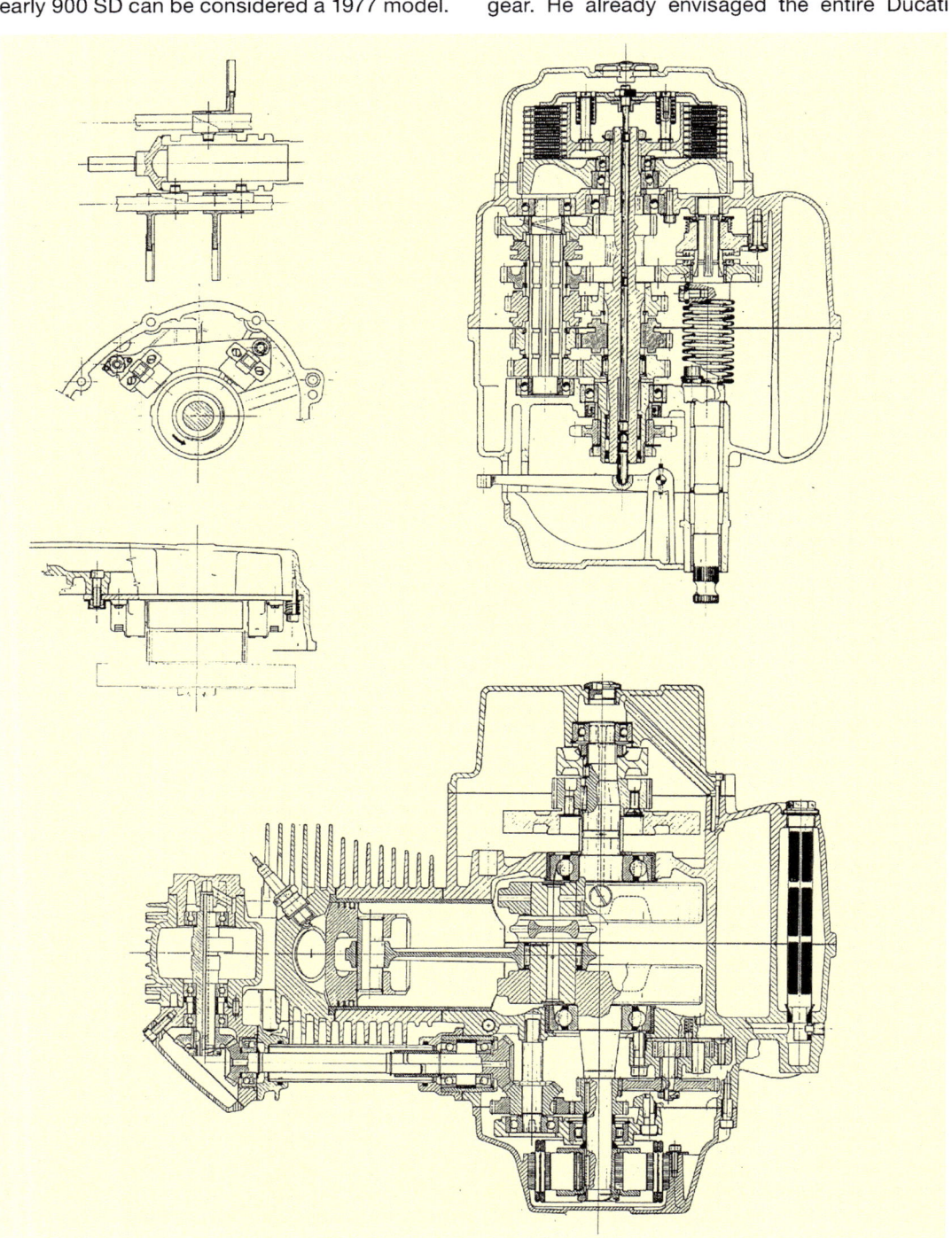

Although the bevel-drive, twin-cylinder engine was essentially as before, the crankshaft and ignition were new for the 900 SD. (Courtesy Ducati Motor)

line-up as desmodromic and, as an all round sports tourer, the 900 SD was pivotal in this quest. Along with desmodromic valves, many other engine updates were incorporated in the 900 SD.

The 900 SD engine numbers began at DM860 900001. This sequence denoted an electric start desmodromic engine and would continue through to the 1984 900 Mike Hailwood Replica. One of the most important updates to the engine was to the crankshaft. While the forged 140mm con-rods were unchanged from the 860 GTS (with a single strengthening web), the big-end bearings were now 23 caged 3x17mm rollers. These provided more bearing surface area and required a larger diameter crankpin (38mm). 1977 models, until engine number 901228, included the earlier crankshaft flywheels for a 36mm pin and a stepped (36-38mm) crankpin. While the new crankshaft didn't solve all the premature big-end failures, the service life on the crankshafts with the smaller diameter roller bearings was vastly improved. With the new crankshaft came larger diameter thrust washers, 36.5x48mm. The gearbox and clutch were the same as for the 860 GTS, but with Allen screws retaining the clutch springs. The 86mm three-ring forged Borgo slipper pistons were now shared with the 900 Super Sport, as were the desmodromic camshafts and valves. The first 900 SDs also had rectangular 900 Super Sport camshaft bearing housings (without '860' markings). While the cylinder head internals were the same as the Super Sport, the cylinder heads only had a narrow (52mm) inlet stud setup for the 32mm Dell'Orto carburettors.

Other improvements included a revised gearshift and selector mechanism and electronic ignition. The gear selector was now located on the left-hand side, underneath the clutch housing. This was superior to the earlier crossover shaft, but the sector pin could break and the selector mechanism wasn't as easily accessible as before. The right-side engine cover included only the clutch rod mechanism. The 900 SD crankcases were also new as the ignition wires now exited through the clutch cover, and there was no need for the hole on the left crankcase under the front engine mount. The electric start cover no longer had '860' markings on it.

The biggest updates were to the electronic ignition and electric start. The Ducati Elettrotecnica ignition system was replaced by a completely new Bosch system with the ignition pickups mounted inside the primary drive cover instead of the crankcases. The flywheel was a 750 style bolt-on type, and the ignition rotor sat on the end of the crankshaft. The ignition pickups ran in the engine oil and, while this wasn't a perfect solution, the system was more reliable than the earlier Ducati Elettrotecnica type.

Functionally, the greatest advantage the Bosch system provided over the Ducati Elettrotecnica was an improved ignition advance. The ignition rotor was shaped so as to provide four stages of advance. At 900rpm advance was 9 degrees, going to 16 degrees at 1800rpm and 28 degrees at 2800rpm. The maximum of 32 degrees advance was reached at 4000rpm. As the system wasn't self generating the engine could no longer be run without a battery. Spark plugs were Champion L88A and the ignition leads were black with, initially, the usual KLG spark plug caps.

While all early 900 SDs still came with a kick-start mechanism, an electric start was standard. All 900 SDs had a 36Ah Yuasa B38 battery and an improved electric start setup. Still using the heavy Marelli MT65B starter motor, the switch and drive system was revised and simplified. The crankshaft starter gear was now independently attached to the crankshaft with a special freewheel bearing inside the flywheel.

Carburetion was by Dell'Orto PHF 32 AD/AS carburettors with black metal air filter boxes and stiff plastic intakes. As with the 1977 860 GTS the white plastic choke lever was fitted on the left-hand side of the instrument panel. There were usual Lafranconi mufflers and dual walled exhaust header pipes, but the right Lafranconi muffler now included a kick-start recess. Gearing on the 900 SD was a 15-tooth engine sprocket with a 38-tooth rear wheel sprocket and 106link ⅝x⅜in chain.

Chassis

The black-painted 900 SD frame was similar to that of the 860 GTS, but included a few modifications. The rear subframe was altered to provide a lower seat height, the front downtubes were bowed with flattened ends, and the front braces were straight instead of curved. Like the 360, the swingarm featured an eccentric chain adjuster at the pivot, but the grease nipple was located in the centre underneath. A side stand mounted on the left front downtube was standard on the 900 SD, and the steering head lock was the usual Neiman type with a separate key. The frame initially carried a DM860SS designation, and the 860 GTS DGM 13715 OM homologation number with a new number sequence. Beginning at 900001, like the Super Sport, these numbers were located on the left-hand side of the frame between the engine mounts (not on the steering head as with the 860 GT/GTS). The silencer homologation plate was mounted on the right-hand side as usual, the numbers now facing the engine. Like the 860 GT this had the designation DM860 S E3 9R-13716.

The 1977 900 SD (until frame number 901173) had a 38mm Ceriani front fork with polished aluminium fork legs and black-painted triple clamps. There were small black 'Ceriani' decals on the lower fork legs. The earliest 900 SD had the longer forks of the 860 GT and GTS, with 608mm fork tubes and 525mm springs. This Ceriani fork also used a shorter (216mm) damping rod. The rear suspension was Marzocchi, and until frame number 900989 these were 300mm. They had chromed-plated springs and a red 'Marzocchi' decal. It wasn't long before Ducati realized that the combination short shock absorbers with a long front fork caused extremely slow steering, so a shorter Ceriani fork was fitted. This was the same length as on the earlier 750 GT, with 580mm tubes, 495mm springs, and 241mm damping rods. After frame number 900900 slightly longer Marzocchi rear shock absorbers replaced the earlier type. These were 12.4in (315mm) and still had chromed springs.

The 900 SD was the first production Ducati to have cast alloy wheels, and in 1977 these were five-spoke, gold-painted Campagnolo with undrilled, four-bolt, 280mm cast-iron discs. There was also a 280mm disc brake on the rear. The brake calipers were Brembo 08, with twin bleed screws, 'Brembo' markings, and plastic pad covers. Two choices of brake pads were available, hard or soft, and the front and rear calipers differed. The front calipers were threaded for a Ceriani fork, while the rear caliper was bolted to the bracket (as for a Marzocchi fork). The Brembo master cylinders front and rear were similar to those of the Super Sport, with the rear master cylinder mounted on the right footpeg and muffler bracket. The rear brake line passed through the plastic rear mudguard. While the Campagnolo front wheel was

The earliest production 900 SD had shorter rear shock absorbers and no 'Tiger' side cover decals.

the same size as on the wire-spoked type (WM3 2.15x18in), the rear wheel rim width was increased to WM4 2.50x18in. The new cast alloy rear also included a cush drive assembly. Both axles were new, the front with a Nyloc nut and without the usual Tommy bar. The tyres on the early 900 SD were Michelin M45, a 3.50H 18in on the front and 4.25/85V 18in on the rear.

Another first for Ducati was the standard fitment of a seven-position, adjustable, hydraulic Paioli steering damper mounted underneath the lower triple clamp and connected to the front frame downtube. All the bodywork was new for the 900 SD. The steel fuel tank held 15-litres, and had the earlier non-locking fuel filler cap. The new Paioli fuel taps were not interconnected and were metal with black plastic tap covers and clear filter bowls on the 1977 bikes. The removable seat base was fibreglass with a distinctive duck tail (or whale tail as it is called), with a lockable rear compartment, and was not hinged at the base as on the 860 GTS. 1977 900 SDs were red with white with 'DUCATI' tank decals and thick white side stripes running

the length of the tank and seat. Most tanks also had a yellow 'Made in Italy' decal. The side covers were ABS with 'SD 900' decals, the left and right a mirror image, with three holes at the rear. There was no tiger decal on the early examples but after around frame number 900450 a tiger decal was added to the side covers on some examples. The tiger decal appears to have been standardised by around frame number 900600. The front and rear mudguards were 'Inox' stainless steel, with a black plastic section behind the rear carburettor. A chromed handrail was fitted on the left; the footpeg rubbers were new, as was the chrome-plated rear brake lever. The chain guard was black.

A completely new instrument panel set the 900 SD apart from earlier Ducatis. The instruments were Nippon Denso, an 8000rpm tachometer on the right and a 220km/h (or 140mph) speedometer on the left. A miles per hour only speedometer was fitted to UK and US 900 SDs. The speedometer used a 25/9 drive and the headlight was a 180mm Bosch 55/60 H4. The 860 style 5/21W CEV taillight was mounted on a black metal bracket. Indicators were chromed plastic CEV, those for the US with side reflectors. The brake and clutch levers were polished aluminium, and the handgrips Japanese to accompany the Nippon Denso throttle. The

horn was changed from Voxbel to black-painted Bosch for the Darmah.

The entire electrical system was updated for the 900 SD. The Bosch three-fuse fusebox and relays were all mounted tightly under the steering head where accessibility was difficult, and the dashboard incorporated an array of warning lights. These were Stand (red), Lights (green), High Beam (blue), Left (orange flasher), Right (orange flasher), Gen (red), Neutral (green). Unfortunately, the switches, particularly for neutral and the side stand, weren't the most reliable. The regulator was now mounted underneath the front of the fuel tank with the Bosch ignition components and there was a new 200W alternator and stator.

The handlebar switches and throttle assembly were also Nippon Denso, the left switch block including lights (off, parking, lights); low, high beam and flash; indicators; and horn. On the right the electric start and engine stop were incorporated into the throttle unit, the single cable throttle including a junction as on the 860 GTS. As 1610 900 SDs were manufactured in 1977 it is difficult to ascertain a cut off point for the 1978 version, but it's convenient to characterise the 1977 model as red and white with a Ceriani front fork and Campagnolo wheels.

Campagnolo wheels and a Ceriani fork typified the 1977 900 SD. (Courtesy Cycle World)

Later 1977 900 SDs had 'Tiger' side cover decals, but there were few other changes.
(Courtesy Ducati Motor)

1977 900 Sport Desmo 'Darmah' distinguishing features
(from engine number DM860 900001-901228; frame number DM860SS 900001-901173)

Engine

New engine number sequence from DM860 900001
New crankcases
Forged 140mm single web con-rods with stepped 36/38mm crankpin
New 200W alternator and stator
900 SS 86mm three-ring forged Borgo pistons
900 SS desmodromic camshafts and valves
Rectangular 900 SS camshaft bearing housings
52mm inlet studs for 32mm Dell'Orto carburettors
Revised gearshift and selector mechanism underneath the clutch housing
New right-side engine cover with clutch rod mechanism
New Bosch ignition with pickups mounted inside the primary drive cover
Kick-start and updated electric start
Electric start cover without '860' markings
Lafranconi mufflers with a kick-start recess

Chassis

New frame number sequence beginning at DM860SS 900001
860 GTS frame homologation number (DGM 13715 OM)
New silencer homologation number E3-9R-13716
New brackets for air filter boxes, regulator, fuel tank, and revised angle of the rear muffler mounting bracket
38mm Ceriani front fork with polished aluminium fork legs and black triple clamps
Marzocchi 300mm shock absorbers until frame number 900989
Marzocchi 315mm shock absorbers after frame number 900900
Five-spoke Campagnolo alloy wheels WM3 2.15x18in and WM4 2.50x18in

Undrilled four bolt 280mm cast-iron brake discs
Brembo 08 brake calipers with twin bleed screws and plastic pad covers
Paioli adjustable hydraulic steering damper
Red with white with 15-litre steel fuel tank, non-locking fuel filler cap, and new Paioli fuel taps
Fibreglass seat with duck (or whale) tail
ABS side covers were ABS with 'SD 900' decals and three holes at the rear
After around frame number 900450 a tiger decal was sometimes on the side cover
Inox stainless steel mudguards with a black plastic section behind the rear carburettor
New footpeg rubbers
Black chain guard
Nippon Denso instruments (US and UK with mph speedometer)
Seven warning lights incorporated in dashboard
White plastic choke lever on dashboard next to speedometer
Polished aluminium brake and clutch levers
Nippon Denso throttle and handgrips
Nippon Denso left handlebar switch
180mm Bosch 55/60 H4 headlight
CEV taillight
CEV turn signals (United States with side reflectors)
Back Bosch horn
Three-fuse fusebox and relays mounted under the steering head
Regulator mounted underneath the front of the fuel tank with the Bosch ignition components

CHAPTER FIVE

1978 – 900 GTS, 900 SD 'DARMAH', 750 AND 900 SUPER SPORT

Although motorcycle production increased significantly during 1977, the viability of Ducati Meccanica as a motorcycle manufacturer was still in the balance during 1978. The decline in the US motorcycle market that began in 1976 continued, and the EFIM Group was now under pressure to utilise the Borgo Panigale plant in more profitable manufacturing enterprises. For several years Ducati had produced a range of light, air-cooled diesel engines, and increased demand for small, stationary diesel engines saw the control of the EFIM group pass to the IRI in July 1978. The IRI also controlled Alitalia and Alfa Romeo at that time. IRI's first step was to

There were only minor changes to the GTS for 1978, and it was now described as a 900 instead of 860. (Courtesy Ducati Motor)

1978 900 GTS distinguishing features (from engine number DM860 854250-855000 approx., frame number DM860S 854200-855000 approx.)

Left side gearshift by crossover shaft
Ducati Elettrotecnica ignition
The six clutch springs were now retained by M5x10mm Allen
  fasteners rather than the M5x12mm slotted screws

Front axle, no longer with a Tommy bar, with nyloc axle nut
New rear 'Inox' stainless steel mudguard with a larger hole for
  the rear brake line
'900' badge with a 'GTS' decal on side covers

install a new diesel engine production line, and gradually reduce the number of motorcycle models available. This year total motorcycle production slipped to 4436, and most of these were 900 bevel-drive twins. While there had always been some inconsistency in specification this year saw an increase in the production irregularity. As Ducati was forced to become more profitable, and motorcycle production almost secondary to that of diesel engines, assembly quality and component specification became more variable.

shaft behind the engine, and the ignition was Ducati Elettrotecnica. Small updates included the six clutch springs retained by M5x10mm Allen fasteners, and a new 20mm front axle, no longer with a Tommy bar on the right-hand side. The M16x1.5x13mm axle nut was now a Nyloc type. Other updates included a new rear 'Inox' stainless steel mudguard with a larger, 18mm hole (with 16mm grommet) for the rear brake line. During 1978 the side cover 900 GTS decals were changed to a '900' badge with a 'GTS' decal.

900 GTS

During 1977 the 860 GTS gained a new designation, 900 GTS, and it continued for 1978 virtually unchanged. Only a small number were produced this year (250) and most 1978 900 GTSs were built towards the end of 1977. Although production of the 900 SD Darmah was well underway the 900 GTS continued with the earlier engine. The left-side gearshift was still operated by a crossover

900 Sport Desmo 'Darmah'

As the 900 SD 'Darmah' was favourably received in the press, Ducati decided to emphasise 900 SD production during 1978. As it was already a well developed model there were only a few updates over the 1977 version. The cylinder head received new, less angular camshaft bearing housings, and new valve guide O-rings. Small updates to improve gear selection included new washers on

A black gold 900 SD was available for 1978. (Courtesy Ducati Motor)

The 900 SD engine for 1978 was unchanged from 1977. (Courtesy Two Wheels)

During 1978 a Marzocchi front fork replaced the Ceriani, with new Brembo brake calipers. The wheels were either Campagnolo or Speedline this year. (Courtesy Tim O'Mahony)

either side of the sector gear (18mm instead of 20mm and 26x1mm instead of 20x0.8mm). The spring detent spacer was also removed, and a new rubber was installed in the alternator plug to prevent oil leaks. From engine number 901229 the con-rods included a straight 38mm crankpin, but the big-end bearings were unchanged. From frame number 901174 the front fork was a 38mm Marzocchi, with polished aluminium fork legs and black-painted triple clamps without any offset. The fork tubes were 600mm, and the Brembo brake

The longer Marzocchi shock absorbers for 1978 also raised the seat height. (Courtesy Two Wheels)

**1978 900 Sport Desmo 'Darmah' distinguishing features
(from engine number DM860 901229-903026; frame number DM860SS 901174-902959)**

New camshaft bearing housings
New valve guide O-rings
New washers on either side of the sector gear
Spring detent spacer removed
New rubber installed in the alternator plug
From engine number 901229 the con-rods included a straight 38mm crankpin

From frame number 901174 38mm Marzocchi front fork
From frame number 901174 new steering damper attachment
Black and gold colours offered alongside the red and white
Gradual change to Speedline wheels
New Neiman steering lock
New Paioli fuel taps

The black and gold colour scheme ultimately proved more popular than the red and white. This 1978 example has engine number 901350. (Courtesy Tim O'Mahony)

calipers were no longer threaded but bolted to the fork. The fork cups were also a new, shallower type, and would soon feature on the Super Sport. At the same time the steering damper attachment was updated to match the new fork.

During 1978 a black and gold colour scheme was offered alongside the red and white. All the side covers now had tiger decals and, coinciding with the black and gold colours, dual, five-spoke, magnesium Speedline wheels gradually replaced the Elektron Campagnolos. These Speedline wheels would prove problematic, however, as they were prone to breakage and corrosion, and they retained a four-bolt brake disc mount. The tyres were mostly Pirelli Gordon MT18, a 3.50H18 on the front, and a 120/90V18 on the rear. Other small updates included metal Paioli fuel taps, still with a clear plastic filter, while the Neiman steering lock was updated to a newer type during the year.

Only a small number of 1978 750 Super Sports were produced and, apart from the Brembo 'Goldline' brake calipers, they were very similar to the 900.

During 1978 the UK importers offered the Darmah as the 900 SD Sport with 40mm carburettors and Contis. However, with the large carburettors and the smaller 52mm cylinder head stud width, this wasn't a totally satisfactory solution.

Although there was some overlap in specification between 1978 and 1979 900 SDs it's convenient to categorize the 1978 900 SD as those with the narrow stud cylinder heads, duck tail (whale) seat, Campagnolo or Speedline wheels, Marzocchi fork, non oleo-pneumatic shock absorbers, and Lafranconi mufflers.

750 and 900 Super Sport

Most Super Sports were 900s for 1978, with only a small number of 750s (30). These were the final Super Sports with the traditional silver and blue

colour scheme and Borrani wire-spoked wheels. Apart from the few built for the UK market in May and June 1978, it's easier to consider the black and gold 900 Super Sport a 1979 model. While 1017 900 Super Sports were produced in 1978, most of these appear to have been built after September in black and gold. As engines were always built and stored before installation in a chassis there was considerable overlap in engine numbers between the last silver 900 Super Sports and the first black examples. This overlap wasn't so evident in frame numbers, though, and a study of engine and frame numbers reveals the 1978 silver and blue 900 Super Sport with Borrani wheels to be one of the rarer 900 Super Sports. Probably around 700 Borrani-wheeled 900 Super Sports were produced as 1978 models.

Engine

For 1978 the engine was based on the Darmah instead of the 860 GT, with the Super Sport engine number series continuing. 900 SS engine numbers began around 087400, overlapping with the earlier Ducati Elettrotecnica ignition engine numbers by several hundred. They finished well beyond some 1979 black and gold bikes at around 088500. While the engine designation was still DM860, many engines also had a stamped 'D' on the right rear crankcase. The 1978 750 Super Sport engine numbers began around 075982, finishing at around 076020. The crankcases were new, with the left-side ignition wire hole cast over, while the 460mm (up from 440mm) crankcase breather hose now incorporated an internal spiral spring. The second breather hose (to the front air filter box) was shorter than before, at 690mm, but the breather chamber was still in the seat base.

Also from the 900 SD was the updated crankshaft with a 38mm crankpin and 23 caged 3x17mm (one-piece) needle roller bearings. The forged con-rods retained the dual strengthening rib around the big-end eye and, until engine number 088026, the crankpin was stepped (36-38mm) for the earlier crank webs. From engine number 088027 there were new crankshaft webs and a straight 38mm crankpin. There was some inconsistency in crankshaft specification, and some 1978 900 Super Sports were fitted with polished 860 single-web con-rods and a straight 36mm pin. Most 1978 900 Super Sports received the new 900 SD camshaft bearing supports (the 750 SS retained the earlier round-case 750 style), and there were new valve guide O-ring seals (now Corteco or 1000760 Viton). Although the alternator rotor was unchanged, there was a new stator for the two-wire 200W alternator. The ignition system was now the Bosch of the 900 SD, as were the Champion L88A spark plugs, black spark plug leads and KLG spark plug caps.

The 1978 Super Sport now featured Bosch electronic ignition and a new clutch cover.

As the Bosch ignition rotor was positioned outside the crankshaft primary gear there was room for a 750-style steel flywheel inside the 32-tooth helical gear. This flywheel was initially identical to that on the 750 but after engine number 088319 was thinner (and lighter). The clutch basket and inner drum were the same as for 1977, but the clutch plate arrangement was changed, and was now the same as the 1975 Super Sport (7 driving and 7 driven plates, 1 inner driven plate with bent tabs facing outwards and an outer driving disc with the tabs facing inwards). 5x20mm Allen screws now retained the clutch springs. The 6-dog gearbox was unchanged but there was a new gear selector drum and selector mechanism on the left, beneath the clutch (as on the 900 SD). The clutch and primary drive cover was also new, with a 24x1.5mm inspection plug, and included the ignition pick-ups and wires. The right-side engine sprocket cover was the same as on the 900 SD, no longer incorporating the gear selector mechanism.

Most 1978 Super Sports had a dual seat.

There were no changes to the Dell'Orto PHF 32A carburettors and air cleaners, and unfiltered PHM 40A carburettors remained an option. The bell mouths were still with wire mesh. 1978 Super Sports also came standard with Lafranconi mufflers, although the long-bracket Contis were an option. Some 1978 Super Sports were fitted with 860 GT or GTS header pipes, and generally the front exhaust nut was drilled and lock wired.

Chassis

The 900 Super Sport continued with the DM860SS number sequence (from around 087500) with the same frame and silencer homologation numbers. 750 Super Sport frame numbers began around number 076225, with the earlier 750 SS homologation numbers. Although the basic frame was unchanged there were revised mounting brackets for the ignition components and footpegs. As the frames were always painted

at the factory after the numbers were stamped there was considerable overlap between the frame numbers of silver and black frames. All 1978 Super Sports came with a steel fuel tank, and there were three types of fuel tap fitted. Some had the early Paioli (Brev Orlandi type), others a metal Paioli that incorporated a small plastic fuel filter, and other examples a grey plastic Paioli without the filter. Sometimes there was a 'MADE IN ITALY' decal on the tank, either the early bright yellow or the later gold type.

While both the previous solo and dual seats were specified, most 1978 Super Sports had a dual seat and 750 GT passenger footpegs. The fibreglass front mudguard was reshaped slightly at the front, and the rear mudguard on all models that of the 1977 US 900 Super Sport. The fairing was also that of the 1977 US version, with a slightly larger opening for the headlamp, and different fairing support brackets. The front screws were also mounted closer together as on the US 1977 version. Some Super Sports came with fairing-mounted rear-view mirrors, and a top fairing support, but these were probably fitted by dealers or distributors as they don't appear in official material.

The Marzocchi front fork now included reshaped fork seal dust covers, while the front axle Tommy bar was removed and the axle nut was now a nyloc. The 310mm Marzocchi shock absorbers were also unchanged, but the top Silentbloc was a 10x25x22mm (instead of 12x25x22) without the extra bush. While the 1978 silver Super Sport is characterised by Borrani wheels, at least one silver and blue 900 was produced with magnesium Speedline wheels as it is pictured in the 1978 spare parts catalogue. It is possible other silver 1978 900 Super Sports had Speedline wheels but unlikely. The 900 Super Sport continued with the 08 Brembo brake calipers with machined bodies, while the few 1978 750 Super Sports came with Brembo 'Goldline' 08 calipers. These had a single bleed nipple and 'BREMBO' emblems, but still no pad covers. The tyres on 1978 Super Sports were generally Michelin M45.

There was a new set of clip-on handlebars, ostensibly identical to the 1977 version but for the left switch mount. The black levers and Verlicchi handgrips were also the same, but the black clutch lever support now included a threaded fitting for a rear-view mirror. Accompanying the revised left-side gear shift was an updated footpeg and lever setup. The steel footpegs were folding on both sides, with a finer metric 12x1mm thread than the similar 1975 Super Sport pegs. The linkages included a combination of the earlier

7mm clevis pin and a balljoint, and the new steel levers had two holes. Other updates for 1978 included new indicator mounting brackets, a new frame-mounted headlamp support, and a longer centre stand. While the rider's footpeg thread was now metric the muffler bolts and passenger pegs (if fitted) were still $7/16$in UNF.

The wiring on the 1978 Super Sport was similar to that of the 900 GTS, with a small Bosch fusebox and the flash relay mounted on the frame. The Bosch fusebox cover was retained by a small screw. Most of the electrical equipment was CEV, including the left handlebar switch. Most 1978 900 Super Sports still had the chrome-plated steel Tommaselli Daytona 2C twin cable throttle, but this was gradually changed during the year to a plastic Verlicchi.

For 1978 the gearshift linkage was improved.

There was a new CEV five-light dashboard for 1978.

1978 Super Sports came with either Smiths or Veglia instruments. Miles per hour speedometers were now supplied by both manufacturers, the type fitted depending on supply at that time. There was also a new dashboard, with five warning lights and a central ignition key, but with a white line highlighting these components. The lights were CEV rather than Aprilia. The headlight was also CEV, as was the large taillight. The metal taillight bracket and metal strengthening plate in the rear mudguard were similar to the 1977 US Super Sport. The turn signals were also chrome plastic CEV, with US examples including side reflectors, while the horn for 1978 was still a single Voxbell.

1978 750 Super Sport distinguishing features (from engine number DM750 075982-076020 approx., frame number DM750SS 076225-076270 approx.)
1978 900 Super Sport distinguishing features (from engine number DM860 087400-088500 approx. frame number DM860SS 087500-088100 approx.)

Engine
New crankcases with the left side ignition wire hole cast over
Crankshaft with 38mm crankpin and caged needle roller bearings
Until engine number 088026 crankpin stepped (36-38mm)
From engine number 088027 straight 38mm crankpin
750 flywheel until engine number 088318, after 088319 a thinner flywheel fitted
New stator for the two-wire 200-watt alternator
460mm crankcase breather hose now incorporated an internal spiral spring
690mm second breather hose
Clutch plate arrangement as for 1975 Super Sport
5x20mm Allen screws retained the clutch springs
New gear selector drum and selector mechanism on the left, beneath the clutch
New clutch and primary drive cover with a 24x1.5mm inspection plug
Right side engine cover no longer incorporated the gear selector mechanism
Most 900s with new 900 SD camshaft bearing supports
New valve guide O-ring seals
Bosch ignition

Chassis
Reshaped front mudguard
Rear mudguard as for 1977 US 900 Super Sport
Fairing with slightly larger headlamp opening
Reshaped fork seal dust covers

New front axle and axle nut
900 SS with 08 Brembo brake calipers with machined bodies and 2 bleed nipples
750 SS with Brembo "Goldline" 08 calipers with single bleed nipple
Top shock absorber Silentbloc 10x25x22mm without a bush.
Clutch lever support included a threaded fitting for a rear view mirror
Folding steel footpegs with finer Metric 12x1mm thread
Foot pedal linkages included 7mm clevis pin and a balljoint
New indicator mounting brackets
New frame-mounted headlamp support
New front fairing brackets with mounting screws closer together
Longer centre stand
New wiring with a Bosch fuse box and the flash relay mounted on the frame
CEV left handlebar switch
Most with Tommaselli Daytona 2C chrome throttle
Smiths or Veglia instruments
New dashboard with five CEV warning lights and a central ignition key
CEV headlight and larger CEV taillight.
Metal taillight bracket and metal strengthening plate in the rear mudguard
CEV turn signals
Voxbell horn

---

900 Super Sport UK version

Shortly before Mike Hailwood's TT F1 victory at the Isle of Man Ducati built a 900 Super Sport in black and gold, with Speedline alloy wheels, specifically for the British market. Production began in May 1978 and it was announced in *The Motor Cycle* on 24 June. Most were fitted with 40mm carburettors, Conti mufflers, a dual seat, and Smiths instruments. One test example subsequently appeared in a number of British motorcycle magazines and was shown at the Earls Court show in August. Ostensibly the British black and gold 900 Super Sport was a regular 1978 900 Super Sport with a black frame, black and gold colours, and Speedline magnesium wheels in place of the Borrani. The drilled discs were the four-bolt type and the rear disc the same 280mm as the front. These 900 Super Sports included a different rear brake caliper support plate for the larger disc. The gold decals were unique to this version, and the colour scheme was considered limited edition as the gold decals were never offered as spare parts. When the black and gold Super Sport went into series production in September 1978 it had decals patterned on the silver and blue SS. It is difficult to ascertain the number of early black and gold examples built with specific graphics for the UK market but it would be very few. The numbers of known examples fall within quite a close range; with engine numbers between DM860 088200-088350 approx., and frame numbers from DM860SS 087850-088000 approx. This indicates production was in one batch, 100 to 150 were built, and they overlapped with the last blue and silver 900 Super Sport.

Racing the 1978 Super Sport

1978 was characterised by significant racing success when Mike Hailwood won the F1 TT at the Isle of Man TT, but the NCR racing machines were only loosely related to their production cousins. Ducati continued to field an endurance racing team and also prepared a stock 900 SS for the Silhouette class. While the prototype endurance racers were unsuccessful this year, Salvador Canellas and Benjamin Grau won the Silhouette class at the 24 Hour race at Le Mans, on April 22-23. On a modified 900 SS they averaged 125.265km/h. This machine was ostensibly a production 900 Super Sport with a race-prepared engine and wider Campagnolo wheels to accept racing tyres. The mufflers were Conti, with special header pipes to increase ground clearance, and the 40mm carburettors breathed through air cleaners. A second machine was ridden by Jose Mallol, expiring on the finish line. These NCR-prepared 900 Super Sports were also raced by Sauro Pazzaglia and Giovanni Mariannini in some Italian events during 1978.

A limited edition black and gold 900 Super Sport was produced during 1978. This was primarily for the UK market.

Benjamin Grau and Salvador Canellas rode this 900 Super Sport to victory in the Silhouette class of the Le Mans 24-Hour race in 1978.
(Courtesy Ducati Motor)

1978 900 Super Sport UK black and gold version distinguishing features (from engine number DM860 082000-088350 approx.; frame number DM860SS 087850-088000 approx.)

Black painted frame
Black bodywork
White 'DUCATI' decals on the fuel tank
Large central gold fuel tank decal and two lower gold stripes

Gold decals on side covers and seat
Speedline magnesium wheels with four-bolt 280mm discs
Most with Smiths instruments
Black air filter boxes on those bikes with air filters

CHAPTER SIX

1979 – 900 SUPER SPORT, GTS, SPORT DESMO & SUPER SPORT DESMO 'DARMAH'

Although riding a wave of publicity following Mike Hailwood's spectacular victory in the Isle of Man Formula 1 TT, difficulties continued at Borgo Panigale during 1979. Ing. Vittorio Scafetti was installed by the EFIM Group as the new general manager during 1978, and he didn't support an increase in motorcycle development. Under his control there was a preoccupation with diesel engines and only 3463 motorcycles were built in 1979, most 900 bevel-drive twins. The parallel twins and 125 two-stroke were gradually discontinued in preparation for the new Pantah. As this production number includes motorcycles built after September 1979 as 1980 models, only a relatively small number of motorcycles were built as 1979 models.

The 1979 900 Super Sport had decals patterned on the earlier silver bikes, and Speedline wheels. (Courtesy Ducati Motor)

900 Super Sport

There was no 750 Super Sport this year, and the success of the black and gold 900 Super Sport in the UK during 1978 saw this form the basis of the 900 Super Sport for all markets in 1979. From September 1978, the black and gold 900 Super Sport with cast alloy wheels replaced the traditional silver and blue Super Sport as a 1979 model. Although very similar to the limited edition British market 900 SS of 1978 there were a few updates.

Engine

As engines were always built separately and stored in racks, engine numbers for the 1979 900 Super Sport overlapped considerably with those of 1978. Numbers began around DM860 088300, with only a few small changes to the engine specification from 1978. After engine number 088319 a thinner, and lighter, flywheel was fitted and, during 1979, the gear selector drum detent spring, peg and screw in the rear of the left crankcase were modified. There was also a new gearbox sprocket retaining nut. Other small updates for 1979 included a new tachometer drive O-ring seal, and an additional thrust washer on the gearbox main shaft. During 1979 Pantah-style metal alternator and ignition wire ring nuts replaced the brittle Bakelite type

that had been fitted since the first 750 GT. There were also new kick-start and selector shaft oil seals (Nadella ET1218 and 2026). The alternator rotor and stator were now the same as those on the 1975 900 SS. Most 900 Super Sports were still fitted with 32mm carburettors as standard, the carburettors changing to Dell'Orto PHF 32 C from April 1979 (with slightly revised jetting). With the new carburettors were Bosch W7B (W175T35) spark plugs. The air filter boxes were unchanged but were painted black to match the frame. The aluminium intake manifolds for PHF 32C carburettors also included an O-ring seal. Lafranconi mufflers were initially fitted as standard equipment, replaced during the year by Silentiums. Although the right Lafranconi sometimes didn't have a kick-start recess, the right Silentium muffler included a kick-start indent. The Dell'Orto PHM 40A carburettor and Conti muffler option remained, and, during 1979, the mesh on the bell mouths changed from wire to aluminium.

Chassis

The black-painted frame continued with the same number sequence and homologation numbers as before. As with engine numbers there was considerable overlap in frame numbers between the silver 1978 and black 1979 versions. Frame numbers began around 087900, and there were

900 Super Sport engines on the test bench at the factory in 1979 before installation in a chassis. Note the gear gazers to check oil supply. (Courtesy Two Wheels)

1979 900 Super Sport distinguishing features (from engine number DM860 088300-089390 approx., frame number DM860SS 087900-089300 approx.)

Engine

After engine number 088319 a thinner flywheel was fitted
During 1979, gear selector drum detent spring, peg and
  screw modified
New gearbox sprocket retaining nut
New tachometer drive O-ring seal
Additional thrust washer on the gearbox main shaft
Metal alternator and ignition wire ring nuts
New kick-start and selector shaft oil seals
Bosch W7B (W175T35) spark plugs
Dell'Orto PHF 32 C carburettors
Aluminium intake manifolds with O-ring seal
Lafranconi mufflers replaced during 1979 by Silentiums
Dell'Orto PHM 40A carburettors with aluminium mesh
  bell mouths

Chassis

Black-painted frame
Black bodywork with gold decals
Grease nipple on swingarm
Brembo 08 brake calipers with twin bleed screws and
  machined bodies
280mm rear disc and new rear brake caliper support plate
Speedline cast magnesium wheels with four-bolt disc mount
CEV switches
Five-light dashboard with mostly Veglia instruments
Voxbell horn
Some still with a Tommaselli Daytona 2C throttle

large discrepancies between engine and frame numbers during this period. All the bodywork was now painted black, with gold decals. These decals were identical in design to the earlier blue and included a gold 'DUCATI' tank logo. The steel fuel tank was the same as for 1978, and most of the fuel taps Paioli with the clear bowl underneath. These taps retained the earlier threaded fitting and still included a linking tube underneath the tank. The side cover decals were white and gold and, as before, there was a choice of a single or dual seat. During 1979 the swingarm gained a grease nipple.

The Marzocchi fork and shock absorbers were unchanged, and the 1979 Super Sport was fitted with the earlier Brembo 08 brake calipers with twin bleed screws and machined bodies. As on the 1978 UK black and gold special edition the drilled 280mm rear disc was identical to the front, and required a new, aluminium, rear brake caliper support plate. The most obvious update was the replacement of the Borrani, alloy-rimmed, wire-spoked wheels with gold-painted, five-spoke, 18in Speedline cast magnesium wheels. The only practical advantage offered by the Speedline wheels was an increase in the rear rim size (to WM4; 2.5in). The Speedline wheels featured a four-bolt brake disc mount.

The tyres were still Michelin M45 but sometimes Pirelli Phantom, a 100/90V18 MT29 on the front and a 110/90V18 MT28 on the rear. All the electrical equipment and CEV switchgear was carried over from 1978, including the five-light

dashboard and Voxbell horn. The throttle was still sometimes a chrome-plated Tommaselli Daytona 2C, but during this period there was a gradual shift to the plastic Verlicchi. Most of the instruments were Veglia during 1979, the tachometer with an 8000rpm redline, and the speedometer without a trip reset. The black and gold 900 Super Sport was undoubtedly one of Ducati's finer styling efforts and would continue for 1980 with minimal updates.

900 GTS

This year saw the end of the 900 GTS and the valve spring Ducati. After 1979 all Ducatis were fitted with cast alloy wheels and desmodromic valves. Seen as unfashionable, the 900 GTS was quietly phased out. Only 150 were produced, and this rare model was the quintessential 860. Apart from the valve spring cylinder heads the engine was the same as the 900 SD, with the same improved left-side gear shift and Bosch ignition. Along with Bosch WM7 spark plugs as fitted to all 900s, this year the 900 GTS had Dell'Orto PHF 32 CD and CS carburettors. The Paioli metal fuel taps were from the 1977 900 SD, and the frame was different to accommodate the brackets for the Bosch ignition coils and relocated horn. The rear brake plate also gained two inspection holes as required by the US DOT to check rear brake lining wear. In other respects the 900 GTS was as for 1978, with Smiths instruments, CEV switches, Tommaselli throttle,

The small number of 1979 900 GTSs featured Bosch ignition and the 900 SD crankshaft. (Courtesy Nico Georgeoglou)

Marzocchi suspension, and Radaelli wheels. While most of these 900 GTSs had Lafranconi mufflers (either with or without a kick-start recess), some of the very last examples were fitted with Silentium mufflers. Some of the last tank badges were also slightly different, with black/silver/black lettering instead of silver/black/silver.

900 Sport Desmo 'Darmah'

As the 900 SD was Ducati's primary model during 1979 it received a number of updates. On 25 January 1979, in a note to importers and concessionaires abroad, Ducati released details of the 1979 900 SD. From engine number 903027 the

The Smiths instruments and CEV dashboard were unchanged from 1978 on the 1979 900 GTS. (Courtesy Nico Georgeoglou)

The Tommaselli throttle with electric start was unique to the 1978 and 1979 900 GTS. (Courtesy Dennis Milani)

The rear drum brake hub included two inspection holes for 1979. (Courtesy Nico Georgeoglou)

The under-seat layout of the 900 GTS was more neatly executed than on many other Ducatis. (Courtesy Nico Georgeoglou)

Racing during 1979

Apart from production events and Silhouette Class endurance racing, until 1979 most successful bevel-twin racing machines were based on the 750 round-case. The factory (NCR) endurance and TTF1 racers were both based on the round-case, but with special narrow, sand-cast crankcases with a spin-on oil filter in the sump. For 1979 the TT F1 regulations were changed, now requiring production-based engines. As the special sand-cast narrow crankcases with the oil filter were no longer allowed the engine was now based on the standard die-cast, square-case 900 SS, without a dry clutch, and remained at 864cc. Ducati was ecstatic after the 1978 TTF1 result and offered Mike Hailwood full factory support for 1979. An all new Formula 1 machine was produced, but was delayed, and it was only two weeks before the TT that the official practice session was held at Misano.

When Hailwood next tested the factory bike he found the handling unsatisfactory. (Courtesy Ducati Motor)

The 1979 factory F1 bike featured a box-section swingarm and special exhaust. This was the first form, as it appeared at the test at Misano. (Courtesy Ducati Motor)

The 1979 F1 machine featured a new Daspa frame, altered fairing shape, and a revised tail section. This frame not only raised the engine to give more ground clearance but the steering head angle was steepened to 29½°. The bikes also had a square-section swingarm to allow for a wider rear tyre, and a high routed left exhaust pipe. At the official practice session at Misano Hailwood's bike was fitted with a reverse direction gearshift by mistake and he crashed towards the end of the two-day test session after inadvertently selecting the wrong gear. Escaping with two cracked ribs, his crash made front page news in Italy and Ducati's director Scafetti decided not to send the bike to the Isle of Man. Worried about insurance liability he agreed to sell the bike to Steve Wynne of Sports Motorcycles in Manchester.

As Hailwood damaged one of the two F1 machines in a crash during testing at Misano, only one F1 (with a spare engine) was sent to the Isle of Man for Hailwood. It arrived only a few days before the race, along with factory mechanics Franco Farnè, Rino Caracchi, and development engineer Renzo Neri. Despite this factory involvement, the 1979 F1

machine was vastly inferior to that of the previous year. Not only down on power, it handled so poorly that Steve Wynne sent for Roger Nicholls' 1978 machine, then on display in the Coburn and Hughes showroom. Although not strictly legal, at the instigation of Ducati, Wynne installed the 1978 model frame with narrower round-section swingarm.

Even with the 1978 frame the F1 bike was disappointing. In practice Hailwood could only manage a lap at 105.88mph, although he felt he was going much faster than the previous year. In the Formula 1 race he lost fifth gear, the battery carrier broke, and an exhaust pipe began to fall off. Hailwood stopped at Hilberry to reconnect the battery and still finished a creditable fifth, at an average speed of 106.06mph with a fastest lap of 109.45mph. So disillusioned was Hailwood with the F1 machine he decided not to race it at any of the post-TT meetings. Hailwood said later that he felt Ducati had let him down in 1979.

Hailwood on his way to fifth place in the 1979 TT F1 race.

1979 900 GTS distinguishing features (from engine number DM860 855000-855200 approx., frame number DM860S 855000-855200 approx.)

900 SD-based engine with Bosch ignition and updated crankshaft
Gearshift and selector beneath clutch drum
Bosch WM7 spark plugs

Dell'Orto PHF 32 CD and CS carburettors
Rear brake with 2 inspection holes
Some with different tank badges

cylinder heads were standardised to those of the 900 Super Sport (with 58mm studs). This allowed 40mm Dell'Orto carburettors to bolt straight on, with a significant performance increase if used with Conti mufflers. The larger carburettors required new intake manifolds, but on the 900 SD these were the same front and rear (900 Super Sport front) to allow room for the larger battery. There was also a new tachometer drive and cover for the front cylinder. In April 1979 the 900 SD received revised carburettors to meet new emissions requirements. The Dell'Orto PHF 32 CD and CS carburettors had different jetting and throttle slides, as well as tamperproof air mixture screws. Along with the new carburettors were Bosch W7B spark plugs. There were also new oil seals for the neutral indicator and kick-start shafts (Nadella ET1218 and Nadella ET2026).

From frame number 902960 the 315mm Marzocchi shock absorbers were changed to a new 330mm oleo-pneumatic type with a remote

reservoir. These now had black, instead of chrome-plated, springs. This update also included a longer centre stand (275mm instead of 260mm) and 55mm spring spacers were installed in the front fork. Sometime soon after the installation of the new shock absorbers there was a new dual seat with more padding and a flip-up rear cover for a tool box. The colours were still red with white stripes or black with gold stripes. 900 SDs destined for the UK and Australia (left-side road use) also received a new Bosch headlight with the correct low beam pattern. The Nippon Denso speedometer for both mph and km/h included markings for both, with two types available. On one the km/h predominated and the other mph. Sometime after frame number 902960 Silentium mufflers replaced the Lafranconis. Although announced in the January technical release the Silentium mufflers took some time to appear, as the author's 1979 900 SD (frame number 903596) had Lafranconi mufflers. The right Lafranconi muffler

On the 1979 900 GTS the sprocket cover no longer incorporated the gear selector mechanism. (Courtesy Nico Georgeoglou)

DUCATI 900
SPORT - DESMO "DARMAH"

For 1979 the 900 SD received a new seat, and Silentium mufflers replaced the Lafranconis. (Courtesy Rob van Klootwijk)

often didn't include the kick-start cutaway, but the Silentium right muffler did. The Silentium mufflers also required a new silencer homologation and carried a plate with the numbers E3 9R-35869. This was now mounted with the top facing towards the side cover. At some stage during 1979 there were also new Paioli fuel taps, with grey plastic taps and no filter bowl.

Although there was some inconsistency in

the specification of the 1979 900 SD this model can be categorised as having oleo-pneumatic chock absorbers, Speedline wheels, and a flip-up seat. Most 1979 900 SDs were built early in the model year, alongside the 900 SSD that shared engine and frame numbers. While the 900 SSD didn't have a kick-start, the 1979 900 SD engine retained a kick-start and the mufflers were generally Lafranconi. The frame numbers

1979 900 SD 'Darmah' distinguishing features (from engine number DM860 903027-903761, frame number DM860SS 902960-903800 approx.)

From engine number 903027 cylinder heads with 58mm studs
Bosch WM7 spark plugs
Dell'Orto PHF 32 CD and CS carburettors
Engine with kick-start
New neutral indicator and kick-start shaft oil seals
From frame number 902960 oleo-pneumatic 330mm Marzocchi shock absorbers
From frame number 902960 a longer centre stand fitted

From frame number 902960 55mm spring spacers fitted to the front fork
New Paioli fuel taps
New dual seat with flip-up cover
Mostly with Lafranconi mufflers but some Silentium
New Nippon Denso speedometer with both mph and km/h markings

continued the DM860SS 900000 sequence (finishing around 903800) with a DGM 13715 OM homologation number.

900 Super Sport Desmo 'Darmah'

By 1979 Ducati saw the most cost effective way to increase sales was through a proliferation of new models based on existing platforms. Two models benefited from this approach, the forthcoming Mike Hailwood Replica, and the 900 Super Sport Desmo 'Darmah'. With over 3300 produced until 1979, the 900 SD was Ducati's most popular model over that period and it seemed logical to expand on that success. The 900 SD was a brilliant combination of an electric start desmodromic 860cc engine in a sport touring chassis, with high quality Japanese and German electrical components. Ducati then saw an opening for a Super Sport based on the Darmah, and the 900 SSD was released at the Bologna Show in October 1978. Combining the

900 SD engine and chassis with a Super Sport riding position and fairing produced an extremely attractive machine. The 900 SSD may not have been as lean and lithe as the regular Super Sport, but it was one of the more attractive machines to emanate from Borgo Panigale. Functionally it gave little away to its race-bred namesake and shared many higher quality components with the SD. Unlike some other new models the 900 SSD went into production almost immediately, with the first 200 examples rolling out of the factory late in 1978 as 1979 examples. A further 409 were built in 1979, but some of these were 1980 models made after September 1979.

Engine

One of the reasons the 900 SSD was implemented so quickly was that the entire engine and drive train was shared with the 900 SD that was already in production. The engine number sequence was shared with the 900 SD, but the 900 SSD

The 900 SSD endeavoured to combine the sporting attributes of the 900 SS with the user-friendly nature of the 900 SD. It was the first 900 Ducati without a kick-start. (Courtesy Ducati Motor)

didn't have a kick-start. The first non-kick-start 900 SD engine was DM860 903762 but the 900 SSD began sometime earlier than this, around 903400. A plug was inserted in the right cover and there were new crankcases. At the same time an additional 7x8x13mm locating bush was inserted between the crankcases and alternator cover. The owners' manual states the compression ratio as 9.5:1 (compared to 9.3:1 for the 900 SD) but according to the parts catalogue there was no difference in engine specification between the 900 SD and 900 SSD.

After engine number 903027, all 900 SSD engines had Super Sport cylinder heads with 58mm wide inlet manifold studs. There were anomalies, and some 900 SSDs had earlier cylinder heads with 52mm studs. The carburettors were Dell'Orto PHF 32C, with 900 SD black-painted air filter boxes and plastic intakes. Also shared with the 900 SD was the exhaust system, with dual-walled header pipes and Lafranconi mufflers. Some Lafranconis also had the kick-start indent (although there was no kickstart fitted) and all mufflers became Silentium during 1979.

Chassis

With the exception of brackets for the steering head-mounted headlight and fairing support, and the rear-set footpegs, the black-painted frame and swingarm were identical to that of the 900 SD. Initially the frame designation was still DM860SS, with the earlier DGM 13715 OM homologation number. Frame numbers began around 903100, finishing around 903800 for 1979. Although most early 900 SSDs had a DM860SS frame designation, the example pictured in the July 1979 owners' manual has a DM900SD frame, with a DGM 19139 OM homologation number. This also features an early frame number (903160) so there was obviously some inconsistency in frame stamping. There was also, sometimes, a silencer homologation plate on the right, near the swingarm pivot, with the numbers for either Lafranconi (E3 9R 13716) or Silentium mufflers (E3 9R-35869).

While the 900 SD featured a revised seat for 1979, the 900 SSD retained the earlier Tartarini seat. The paintwork was a distinctive two-tone

On the 900 SSD the rear brake master cylinder was mounted higher and the brake line went through the right-hand side cover. (Courtesy Nico Georgeoglou)

All 900 SSDs had six-bolt drilled discs with aluminium carriers. (Courtesy Nico Georgeoglou)

blue, with a 900 SD fuel tank and Super Sport-style half fairing. The steel tank featured white 'DUCATI' lettering, with dark blue accents. The seat base also included dark blue accent decals, and a white 'DARMAH' decal on each side of the tail. Although the half fairing looked similar in design to that of the Super Sport, it was larger and shaped differently. The Ballanti Roberto plexiglass screen featured a black plastic beading, and there was no upper cross brace. Around the headlamp were dark blue decals, with a 'DESMO' decal on each side of the fairing lowers.

The ABS side covers featured the tiger decal and white 'SS 900' decals, and the right side cover was different. It didn't have three holes in the rear as the rear brake hose passed through a diagonal cut in the rear of the cover. The rear master cylinder was located higher on the bracket, and the master cylinder banjo almost touched the side cover. The brake hose ran through the side cover across to the left, in front of the plastic mudguard instead of through as on the 900 SD. The hole in the plastic mudguard was blanked off on the 900 SSD. The 900 SSD rear brake hose was also longer (370mm instead of 320mm).

The suspension on the 900 SSD was identical to that on the 900 SD, with a 38mm Marzocchi front fork with polished aluminium fork legs, and black-painted triple clamps. The top triple clamp was without handlebar mounts. The rear shock absorbers were Marzocchi oleo-pneumatic 330mm as on the 900 SD.

The 1979 900 SSD was fitted with magnesium Speedline wheels (same rim sizes as the 900 SD), but unlike those on the 900 SD and 900 SS these featured a six-bolt disc attachment. The drilled 280mm disc rotors had aluminium carriers and were a higher specification disc than the four-bolt type. The tyres were identical to the 900 SD, Pirelli Gordon (3.50H18 and 120/90V18) in 1979. But for the longer rear brake line and shorter top front brake line (280mm) the Brembo braking system was shared with the 900 SD. Two types of brake pad were specified; a soft MF02 and harder MF01. The stainless steel mudguards were similar to those on the 900 SD, but the front was more rounded in shape.

The clip-on handlebars and high rear-set footpegs provided the 900 SSD with a unique riding position. Although they mounted below the top triple clamp, the handlebars were offset forwards and upwards. The rider's folding steel footpegs screwed into lugs welded on the frame. These were high up on the rear, near the bottom of the side cover. The steel gearshift lever was from the 900 SS, but unlike the 900 Super Sport

On the 1979 900 SSD the rider's footpegs were mounted high and rearward. (Courtesy Nico Georgeoglou)

The rear brake lever and footpeg of the early 900 SSD. (Courtesy Nico Georgeoglou)

The cockpit of the 900 SSD included the 900 SD instrument layout and unique, forward offset, clip-on handlebars. (Courtesy Ducati Motor)

1979 900 SSD 'Darmah' distinguishing features (from engine number approx. DM860 903400-903761, frame number DM860 SS or DM900SD 903100-903800 approx.)

900 SD engines without kick-start
Most cylinder heads with 58mm inlet manifold studs
Lafranconi mufflers becoming Silentium
900 SD frame mostly with DM860SS and DGM 13715 OM homologation number
Earlier 900 SD seat, half fairing, and two-tone blue paint
New right side cover with rear brake hose passing through a cut in the rear
Rear master cylinder located higher on the bracket
Hole in the plastic mudguard blanked off
Longer rear and shorter top front brake hoses

Top triple clamp was without handlebar mounts
Speedline wheels with six-bolt disc attachment
Drilled 280mm discs with aluminium carriers
Clip-on handlebars and high rear-set footpegs
900 SS steel gearshift lever with balljoints at either end of the gearshift linkage
Passenger footpegs mounted on a steel support
Instruments and warning lights mounted on the steering head bracket
Nippon Denso speedometer with mph and km/h graduations
Front mudguard more rounded in shape

there was a balljoint at either end of the gearshift linkage. Because of the extreme rear-set location of the rider's footpegs, the passenger footpegs were mounted on a steel support that positioned the pegs further rearward.

Generally the ancillary equipment was shared with the 900 SD. The handlebar levers were polished aluminium, the instruments, switches and throttle Nippon Denso, and the headlamp Bosch. As on the 900 SD the Nippon Denso speedometer included markings for both mph and km/h. Other 900 SD equipment included the Bosch horn, CEV taillight and CEV turn signal indicators. There was also a side stand and centre stand, seven-position Paioli hydraulic steering damper, Neiman steering head lock, and a black chain guard. Completing the frame fittings was a chrome-plated grab handle under the seat on the left. The instruments and warning lights were mounted on the steering head bracket rather than the top triple clamp.

CHAPTER SEVEN

1980 – 900 SS, 900 MHR, 900 SD, 900 SSD

During 1980 Finmeccanica, of which Ducati was a part, moved from the EFIM to the VM Group. Although the VM Group was also preoccupied with diesel engines there was an improvement in the motorcycle situation. Along with the next generation V-Twin, the Pantah, the 900 Mike Hailwood Replica finally went into production, commencing production after September 1979 as a 1980 model. Production increased 28 per cent over 1979, to 4452 motorcycles.

900 Mike Hailwood Replica (first series)

When the great motorcycle racer Mike Hailwood came out of semi-retirement at the age of 38 to win the 1978 Isle of Man Formula One race on an NCR Ducati, the company saw another opportunity to market a race replica. There was talk of a production Mike Hailwood Replica immediately after the race in early June 1978, but it was over

The production 900 Mike Hailwood Replica was first displayed at the London Motorcycle Show in August 1979. (Courtesy Two Wheels)

12 months before a production version appeared. This delay wasn't unexpected as Ducati had a history of delaying production race replicas. After promising a production version of the Imola 200 race-winning desmodromic 750 in April 1972, it took two years before the eventual 750 Super Sport became available. The 750 Super Sport was a relatively close replica of the Imola racer, but when the Mike Hailwood Replica appeared it was very much a cosmetic adaptation of the 900 Super Sport. Despite its flaws the Mike Hailwood Replica was destined to become Ducati's most popular model in the early 1980s, lasting beyond the demise of the Super Sport.

Initially titled the 900 Replica, it was shown for the first time at the Earls Court Motorcycle Show in London in August 1979. Unfortunately, by this time, some of the euphoria surrounding the 1978 victory had waned. Hailwood had finished an unspectacular fifth in the 1979 Isle of Man Formula One race, on an inferior machine to that of 1978. Undeterred, Ducati proceeded with the production of a series of 200, each with a certificate of authenticity. The first 900 Replica was produced primarily for the British market but small numbers were sold in other European countries. It was undoubtedly intended to be produced in small numbers as some of the components were crudely executed.

Engine

Through until the end of the kick-start series of Mike Hailwood Replica in 1983 the engine was identical to the 900 Super Sport. The engine number sequence was shared, as were the updates that occurred over the next few years. Engine numbers for the 1980 Replica began at around DM860 089390, continuing until around 090100. The claimed power for the 900 Replica was 80 horsepower at 7000rpm with 40mm carburettors and Conti mufflers. While there were no changes in specification from the 900 SS, two sets of larger valves were listed as an option for the 900 Replica. These were either a 42mm inlet and 38mm exhaust, or a 44mm inlet and 40mm exhaust.

Only Dell'Orto PHM 40A carburettors were fitted to the early 900 Replica. These were without chokes or air cleaners and came with the usual plastic bell mouths. Often the bell mouths had wire gauze filters but these became aluminium during 1980. Because there were no air filter boxes the

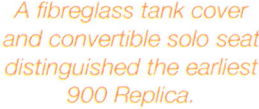

A fibreglass tank cover and convertible solo seat distinguished the earliest 900 Replica.

crankcase engine breather fed into a plastic box under the seat through a 255mm tube, and exited via a 500mm tube into a flapper valve attached to the frame under the fuel tank.

Conti mufflers were also fitted to the early 900 Replica, with new exhaust header pipes that routed closer to the engine to enable the fairing to fit more closely. The left pipe now needed to be removed for oil changes or checking, but this was only a minor inconvenience compared to removal of the one-piece fairing.

Chassis

The 900 Replica shared its chassis with the 900 SS but with a few updates. The early 900 Replica frames were stamped DM860SS with DGM 13715 OM homologation. The number series was new, and for some reason was the same series as the 900 SD Darmah, but beginning again at 900001. Apart from various brackets, a different headlamp support, and revised seat mounts, the red-painted Verlicchi frame was the same as that of the Super Sport and not the 900 SD. While there were no brackets for the side covers, there were for the air filter boxes. Because they were fitted with Conti mufflers early 900 Replicas didn't have a silencer homologation plate.

It was mainly the bodywork that set the 900 Replica apart from the Super Sport. The red, white and green colours were inherited from Hailwood's Sports Motorcycle TT1 racer that was sponsored by Castrol. As fibreglass fuel tanks were banned in England, where the first Replica was headed, the first 200 examples came with a rudimentary fibreglass cover (replicating the NCR tank shape) over the regular, black-painted, 18-litre steel fuel tank. Initially it was intended to produce the 900 Replica with a fibreglass fuel tank with a clear strip (à la Imola 750), and at least one example was produced as it appears in publicity material. A solo seat was standard, and converting to a dual seat required substituting a replacement seat pad. Like the fibreglass tank cover, the dual seat setup was seemingly designed as an afterthought. The fuel taps were grey plastic Paioli and not linked. The early Replica was also easy to recognise as the early fuel tank cover decals were mounted very high.

All early 900 Replicas came with a large fibreglass one-piece full fairing, initially without white 'DUCATI' decals. Most early Replicas had small 'Mike Hailwood Replica' decals on either side of the headlamp, but this wasn't universal. The fairing incorporated the front turn signal indicators

and was retained by ten 6x16mm chrome-plated screws. The first versions had different fairing brackets, and an aluminium top cross brace, with a single white stripe separating the red and green. Some examples had two white stripes. The fairing screen was also different to that on the Super Sport, and was retained by nine slot head screws instead of seven. There were no side covers, and the mudguards were red fibreglass.

The 900 Replica had slightly different Marzocchi suspension to the 900 Super Sport. While the 38mm fork was basically identical, it had polished aluminium fork legs with black-painted triple clamps. There was still a small red 'MARZOCCHI' decal at the base of the left fork leg. Because the fairing cross brace attached to the steering head retaining nut there was no friction steering damper. To improve ground clearance the Marzocchi shock absorbers were 20mm longer, at 330mm. These had black springs and a small red decal.

All Replicas were fitted with cast alloy wheels, either Speedline or Campagnolo on the first series. The wheels and 280mm drilled brake discs were identical to those on the 1979 900 Super Sport, and had a four-bolt brake disc attachment. The tyres were Pirelli Phantom, 100/90V18 and 110/90V18, and there was a special 102-link Regina 'Grand Prix–136' $^5/_8$x$^3/_8$in chain for the MHR, with 15- and

This early 900 Replica had a fibreglass fuel tank with a clear strip, as on the earlier Imola racer and 750 Super Sport. (Courtesy Ducati Motor)

36-teeth sprockets. Also shared with the 1979 900 Super Sport were the Brembo 'Goldline' brake calipers, along with the new junction on the bottom triple clamp and a 280mm upper brake hose. The rear brake light switch was situated on the caliper rather than the master cylinder, some alloy rear brake caliper supports were relieved with holes rather than milled. The chrome-plated clip-on handlebars were similar to those of the 1979 900 SS, but with different screw mounts to clear the larger fuel tank. The throttle was a black plastic Verlicchi, the handgrips Verlicchi, and the brake and clutch levers black.

Although the 900 Replica was strongly

1980 900 Replica first series distinguishing features (from engine number DM860 089390-090100 approx, frame number DM860SS 900001-900200)

Dell'Orto PHM 40A carburettors without chokes or air cleaners
Conti mufflers and new exhaust header pipes
DM860SS frame with DGM 13715 OM homologation and 900000 number series
Red-painted frame with different headlamp support and no side covers
No silencer homologation plate
Fibreglass cover over the black-painted steel fuel tank
High decal placement on the fuel tank cover
Standard solo seat with conversion to dual with replacement seat pad
Fibreglass one-piece full fairing, initially without white 'DUCATI' decals
Most with small 'Mike Hailwood Replica' decals on either side of the headlamp
Different fairing brackets to later models
Aluminium fairing top cross brace

Fairing screen retained by nine screws
No side covers, but with red mudguards
Polished aluminium fork legs with black-painted triple clamps
No friction steering damper
330mm Marzocchi shock absorbers
Speedline or Campagnolo wheels
280mm drilled brake discs with four-bolt attachment
Brembo 'Goldline' brake calipers
Rear brake light switch was situated on the caliper rather than the master cylinder
New clip-on handlebars but with different screw mounts to clear the fuel tank
Black plastic Verlicchi throttle
Verlicchi handgrips
Black brake and clutch levers
CEV headlamp, taillight, and direction indicators
Nippon Denso left side handlebar switch and instruments

derived from the 900 Super Sport, some of the equipment was shared with the 900 SSD 'Darmah'. There was a mixture of CEV and Nippon Denso equipment, with a CEV headlamp, taillight, and direction indicators, a Nippon Denso left-side handlebar switch and Nippon Denso instruments. The speedometer was mounted on the left, with the tachometer on the right, with a warning light panel in between. Various types of speedometer were fitted, either km/h and mph, or mph and km/h (as on the 1979 900 SD). As they were intended for the British market most early Replicas had a 140 miles per hour speedometer, often without additional km/h markings.

900 Mike Hailwood Replica (Second 1980 series)

The 900 Replica was immediately successful and the initial batch of was followed by a further 100 towards the end of 1979. 447 similar machines were produced during 1980 bringing the total 1980 Mike Hailwood Replicas to 647. The second 1980 series was essentially the same as the first series, but there was no longer a certificate of authenticity and there were a few updates to the bodywork.

As always with new model series there was some overlap with engine numbers, the second series often using earlier numbers than some of the first series. The final second series 1980 MHRs seems to have been built towards the end of the Model Year as some had engines with significantly later numbers than 900 Super Sports of this period. Engines were still shared with the 900 Super Sport and began at around 089900, through until around 091400. The engines were largely unchanged from 1979, but after January 10, 1980, the crankshaft was unified with the 900 SD and 900 SSD. Kick-start Super Sport engines required a closed bush over the 2mm lubrication hole in the left shaft for the electric start bearing. At the same time the camshaft in the vertical cylinder was changed, with a reducing bush inserted inside the lubrication hole. If the reducing bush was not fitted to these camshafts serious engine damage could result. Other engine updates during 1980 were minor, including a new gearshift spring and detent in the rear crankcase, new countershaft sprocket ring nut, new stop ring for the cylinder head tachometer drive, and Pantah-style alternator and ignition wire plugs. The carburettors were still Dell'Orto PHM 40A and the mufflers Conti.

Most changes were to the bodywork, with a new 24-litre steel fuel tank specifically designed for the 900 Replica. This included a different right fuel tap, and the fuel filler opened the opposite direction (towards the rider). The dual seat was

This second series 900 Mike Hailwood Replica had Campagnolo wheels but most were FPS. The fuel tank was steel and the fairing still one-piece. (Courtesy Two Wheels)

or occasionally Campagnolo. Sometimes the FPS wheels had a six-bolt disc attachment but were generally four-bolt. The six-bolt wheels also included 280mm drilled discs with aluminium carriers. From frame number 900504 the FPS wheels had two 8mm dowels to locate the cush drive to the hub. During 1980 the front fork received black-painted fork legs, with a yellow decal. Some fairings on the last 1980 versions also featured a large 'DUCATI' decal on either side, although the fairing remained one-piece.

900 Super Sport

The 900 Super Sport was largely unchanged for 1980 and, while some gradual updates were incorporated during the year, there was no actual model year delineation. As engines were shared

This new seat was more easily converted to accept a passenger. (Courtesy Ducati Motor)

now easily converted to a solo seat and featured revised upholstery with a 'DUCATI' stamping on the solo seat bump. But for new 6x18mm retaining screws the one-piece fairing was unchanged, and was still with a single large white stripe separating the red and green sections. The Ballanti Roberto fairing screen included plastic beading and there were still no side covers.

On the second series 900 Replica the wheels were mostly aluminium FPS (with polished rims),

The rear-end styling of the 900 Replica was based on the NCR racer. (Courtesy Ducati Motor)

1980 900 Replica second series distinguishing features (from engine number DM860 089900-091400 approx., frame number DM860SS 900201-900750 approx.)

Crankshaft was unified with the 900 SD and 900 SSD
Vertical cylinder camshaft with reducing bush
New gearshift spring and detent in the rear crankcase
New countershaft sprocket ring nut
New stop ring for the cylinder head tachometer drive
Pantah-style alternator and ignition wire plugs
New 24-litre steel fuel tank, new right fuel tap, fuel filler opening opposite way
New seat with solo section and 'DUCATI' stamping on the solo seat bump
6x18mm fairing retaining screws

Fairing screen with plastic beading
Wheels mostly aluminium FPS (with polished rims), or occasionally Campagnolo
Some FPS wheels with six-bolt disc attachment but were generally four-bolt
Six-bolt wheels included 280mm drilled discs with aluminium carriers
From frame number 900504 the FPS wheels had two 8mm dowels to locate the cush drive to the hub
During 1980 the front fork with black-painted fork legs (with yellow decals)

with the 900 MHR the engine number sequence now diverged even more markedly from the frame numbers. Engine numbers for 1980 began around 089390 (as for the 900 MHR), continuing to 090914 by interpolating factory service bulletins. The final engine numbers were significantly lower than the comparable 900 MHR, indicating Super Sports were built earlier in the model year. During 1980 the crankshafts were unified and there was a new

vertical camshaft. Most 1980 900 Super Sports left the factory with PHF 32C carburettors and Silentium mufflers.

The 900 SS chassis and black and gold paint work was also largely unchanged for 1980. Frame numbers began at approximately DM860SS 089300, finishing around 090100. As with the engine numbers there was some overlap with frame numbers between 1980 and 1981 examples. The

The 1980 900 Super Sport was virtually identical to the 1979 version, and most had FPS wheels. This transitional example has early twin bleed Brembo brake calipers and four-bolt discs. (Courtesy Nico Georgeoglou)

silencer homologation plate was changed, with a new number for Silentium mufflers (E3 9R-35869). While most of the equipment was unchanged from 1979 some fuel tanks now had a revised threaded fitting and non-linked grey Paioli fuel taps.

During 1980 the Speedline wheels were changed to FPS, the FPS wheels having polished aluminium rims and either a four-bolt or six-bolt brake disc mount. Later in 1980 some FPS wheels had gold-painted rims. The six-bolt wheel required new brake discs (with aluminium carriers). A problem with the cast rear wheels was a gradual loosening of the cush drive hub and, from frame number 089779, two additional 8mm dowels were added to the flange of the rear FPS wheel. The brake calipers were now mostly Brembo Goldlines with a single bleed nipple that was fitted to the 1978 750 Super Sport. With the Goldline calipers was a revised junction on the lower triple clamp and a 280mm upper rubber brake line. The rear brake light pressure switch also moved from the master cylinder to the caliper.

Other small equipment updates included a black Bosch horn, black plastic Verlicchi throttle, new plastic clutch cable adjuster, Nippon Denso left-side handlebar switch, and smaller diameter (6mm) pins on the gearshift and rear brake linkages. The rear indicator support was longer (290mm instead of 260mm) and there was a new type of Neiman steering head lock.

900 Sport Desmo 'Darmah'

Several changes to the specification of the 900 SD, both to the engine and chassis, occurred

Some 1980 900 Super Sports had FPS wheels with polished rims, Goldline brake calipers, and six-bolt discs.

1980 900 Super Sport distinguishing features (from engine number approx. DM860 089390-090914, frame number DM860SS 089300-090100 approx.)

Crankshaft unified with the 900 SD and 900 SSD

New vertical cylinder camshaft with a reducing bush in lubrication hole

Most with Silentium mufflers and new homologation plate

Black frame and black and gold paintwork

Some fuel tanks with new type non-linked Paioli fuel taps

During 1980 Speedline wheels changed to FPS with polished rims

Later in 1980 some FPS wheels had gold-painted rims

Either a four- or six-bolt disc attachment

Six-bolt wheel with new brake discs

From frame number 089779 two additional 8mm dowels in cush drive

Brembo Goldline brake calipers

New brake junction and 280mm upper rubber brake line

Rear brake light pressure switch moved from the master cylinder to the caliper

Black Bosch horn

Black plastic Verlicchi throttle

New plastic clutch cable adjuster

Nippon Denso left handlebar switch

6mm pins on the gearshift and rear brake linkages

290mm rear indicator support

New Neiman steering head lock

Racing during 1980

By 1980 the bevel-drive Ducati was largely outclassed in endurance racing, and there was no official factory involvement in the Coupe d'Endurance. It was left to privateers to continue its development and provide Ducati with another outstanding victory in the Barcelona 24-hour race at Montjuich. On a modified 900 Super Sport entered in the Silhouette Class by local importer Ricardo Fargas, Jose Mallol and Alejandro Tejedo provided Ducati its first victory in this event since 1975. The bike was only entered as the Barcelona race was also the final round of the Spanish Endurance Championship and no-one expected to defeat the field of Hondas and Kawasakis. Mallol and Tejedo covered 757 laps at 74.12mph (119.3km/h), two laps ahead of the second placed Honda. The team's second bike finished tenth, in the hands of Reyes and Duran. Although based on the square-case 900 Super Sport, the winning bike was highly modified, with an NCR fuel tank and seat unit. The engine was still 864cc, and the exhaust system, a two-into-one, tucked in tightly on the left for maximum ground clearance.

While the 1979 TT was a disaster for Ducati, the company continued to field a 900 F1 racer in Italian TT Formula One

events. Vanes Francini rode a factory racer in the 1980 Italian Regions Trophy TT1 Championship. This machine was also based on the production 900 Super Sport, with FPS (or sometimes Campagnolo) wheels, fully-floating gold series Brembo brakes, and NCR bodywork. The frame was also production-based, with a round-section swingarm. Francini won three races to take the championship.

Vanes Francini won the 1980 TT1 Italian Regions Trophy on a factory 900. (Courtesy Ducati Motor)

during 1980. Most of these updates were to create uniformity between the various bevel-twin models. Coinciding with the release of the 900 SSD and 900 MHR the engine lost the kick-start and there was a new frame number sequence. The colours of black and gold or red and white were unchanged from 1979.

Engine

Engine numbers for the 1980 900 SD began at DM860 903762 when the kick-start and kick-start shaft were removed so the engine was uniform with the 900 SSD. A plug was inserted in the right cover, and there were new crankcases. At the same time an additional 7x8x13mm locating bush was inserted between the crankcases and alternator cover. As with the 900 Super Sport, early in 1980, there was the unification of 900 crankshaft types the 2mm lubrication hole for the freewheel electric start bearing with an open bush. The con-rods were now 900 SS, with a dual rib around the big-end. There was also a new vertical camshaft, with a reducing bush inserted inside the camshaft lubrication hole.

From engine number 904414 there was a shorter gear lever, with a correspondingly shorter sector gear shaft (149mm instead of 134mm). This also required a new clutch cover. This change to the length of the gearshift shaft was brought about to lower the footpeg placement on the 900 SSD that shared engines and frames. During the year the Bakelite alternator and clutch cover plugs were changed to the metal/Bakelite combination of the 500 SL Pantah. The 900 SD also shared the 200W alternator of the 500 SL Pantah.

Chassis

With the release of the 900 Replica for 1980 also using DM860SS frames with 900000 series numbers, there was a new frame number sequence of the 900 SD beginning at 950001. The very first 950000-series frames retained the DM860SS frame designation and DGM 13715 OM frame homologation number but after

Top: The 1980 900 SD mostly featured FPS wheels with polished rims. The mufflers were Silentiums. (Courtesy Ducati Motor)

On the 1980 900 SD the front discs were still undrilled, with a four-bolt mount. The Marzocchi fork legs were polished. (Courtesy Ducati Motor)

around frame number 950500 the designation changed to DM900SD. These frames carried a new homologation number DGM 19139 OM and coincided with engine number 904414. The steering head lock was a new type of Neiman. The wheels were still Speedline on the early 1980 900 SD but they were gradually replaced by aluminium FPS. These FPS wheels had four bolt holes for the solid 280mm cast-iron discs, gold-painted spokes, and polished aluminium rims. Later in 1980 the FPS wheel rims were painted gold to match the spokes. During 1980 some of the aluminium rear brake caliper supports were a different type, with three large holes instead of a milled centre. While the front Marzocchi fork still had polished aluminium fork legs, some of the decals were yellow instead of red. Although many more motorcycles were built during 1980, only 480 were 900 SDs as the emphasis moved

The flip-up seat on the 1980 900 SD was unchanged from 1979. (Courtesy Ducati Motor)

The 1980 900 SD instrument panel was also unchanged from 1979; the speedometer graduated in mph and km/h. (Courtesy Ducati Motor)

1980 900 SD 'Darmah' distinguishing features (from engine number DM860 903762-905167, frame number DM860 SS or DM900SD 950001-951260)

Some with kick-start and later examples without
New crankcases
Additional locating bush between the crankcase and alternator cover
Unified crankshaft with 900 SS with a dual rib con-rods
New vertical camshaft with a lubrication reducing bush
Shorter gear lever from engine number 904414 with a 149mm sector gear shaft
New clutch cover from engine 904414
During the year new alternator and clutch cover plugs fitted
200W alternator shared with 500 SL Pantah
New frame number sequence beginning at 950001

Initially with DM860SS frame designation and DGM13715OM homologation
After around frame number 950500 DM900SD with DG M19139OM
New Neiman steering head lock
Initially Speedline wheels
FPS wheels with four-bolt disc mount and polished aluminium rims during 1980
Later in 1980 the FPS wheel rims were painted gold to match the spokes
Some aluminium rear brake caliper supports with three large holes

The 900 SSD fairing was similar in style to that of the 900 SS but not identical. (Courtesy Ducati Motor)

towards more sporting models. Most 900 SD production went to Australia this year, with 228 examples heading Down Under.

900 Super Sport Desmo 'Darmah'

After a modestly successful introduction in 1979 the 900 SSD continued for 1980 with minor updates. Engines were still shared with the 900 SD, beginning at 903762 through until 905167. As on the 900 SD, after engine number 904415 there was a shorter gearshift shaft and new clutch cover, this approximately coinciding with the frame with the revised footpeg position. Some later number engines were known to have the longer gearshift shaft so there was some overlap. The carburettors remained Dell'Orto PHF 32C and the mufflers Silentium.

The frame received a new frame number designation, homologation number, and number sequence for 1980. This was now from DM900SD 950001 DGM 19139 OM but some early 1980 frames retained the DM860SS designation. During 1980 the Speedline wheels were replaced by aluminium FPS, with polished rims, but the 900 SSD always featured a six-bolt disc attachment. The drilled brake discs with aluminium carriers were unchanged.

Criticism of the riding position led to a redesign of the lever and footpeg layout from frame number 950762. To lower the footpegs and bring them further forward, they were now located on brackets bolted to the frame serrations underneath the swingarm pivot. No longer threaded, the footpegs were retained by two 8x20mm bolts and slotted into the brackets. There was an accompanying shorter gearshift and longer brake control rod and the footpegs had rubbers. The passenger footpegs were repositioned onto the muffler bracket. There were no other changes to the chassis specification apart from a 500 SL Pantah clutch cable adjuster. 900 SSD production was always modest, but in 1980 it exceeded that of the 900 SD, with 705 produced, including 100 for England and 260 for Australia.

All 900 SSDs featured the earlier style 900 SD 'Darmah' seat. (Courtesy Ducati Motor)

The electric start 900 SSD motor was shared with the 900 SD. (Courtesy Ducati Motor)

The wheels for the 1980 900 SSD were FPS, still with the six-bolt drilled discs. (Courtesy Ducati Motor)

The Silentium mufflers and remote reservoir Marzocchi shock absorbers were also shared with the 900 SD. (Courtesy Ducati Motor)

1980 900 SSD 'Darmah' distinguishing features (from engine number DM860 903762-905167, frame number DM860 SS or DM900SD 950001-951260)

After engine number 904415 shorter gearshift shaft and new clutch cover

New frame number sequence beginning at 950001

Initially with DM860SS frame designation and DGM13715OM homologation

After around frame number 950500 DM900SD with DGM19139OM

Aluminium FPS wheels with polished rims and six-bolt disc attachment

Redesigned lever and footpeg layout from frame number 950762

Footpegs with rubbers now located on brackets bolted to the frame serrations

Shorter gearshift and longer brake control rod

Passenger footpegs were repositioned onto the muffler bracket

500 SL Pantah clutch cable adjuster

During 1980 the footpegs were lowered and there were new linkages.

CHAPTER EIGHT

1981 – 900 SS, 900 MHR, 900 SD, 900 SSD

For 1980, Ducati expanded the line-up to include nine models (four parallel twins, four bevel-twins and the 500 Pantah), but many of these proved unprofitable and difficult to sell. In an effort to rationalise production, the model range was cut for 1981. The parallel twins were gradually phased out in favour of the 500 and 600 SL Pantah, and the 900 SSD made way for the 900 Mike Hailwood Replica. For 1981 the emphasis was on increasing the production of established models, and, within the bevel-twin line-up, this was concentrated on the 900 MHR and 900 Super Sport. 1981 was a very good year for bevels, though, as, of the 6838 motorcycles produced during that year, 3474 were bevel-twins. 1981 saw bevel-twin production reach its peak, but, from here onwards, it was a gradual downward slide.

For 1981 the 900 Super Sport came in for its first major re-style since 1976. (Courtesy Ducati Motor)

900 Super Sport

After eight years with minimal development the 900 Super Sport was mildly updated for 1981. This new 900 Super Sport was displayed at the Bologna Show at the end of 1980, and went into production in early 1981. Most of the changes were cosmetic, but unfortunately there was also a decline in quality control as the VM management strove to increase production. 900 Super Sport production was increased to 1165, but undoubtedly a few hundred of these were manufactured after September as 1982 models.

Engine

The 900 Super Sport kick-start engine continued much as before but with some small updates. Examination of service bulletins indicates engine numbers began at 090915 for 1981, through until the end of the six-dog gearbox at number 092920. As always there was inevitably some engine overlap between the 1980, 1981, and 1982 model years, and the same engines were shared with the 900 MHR.

From engine number 090915 (the start of the 1981 model year), the Bosch ignition module connectors and pickups were updated. The connectors were now those of the 500 and 600 SL Pantah. There was a Pantah alternator rotor, combined with the earlier 860 stator. Although the basic design and specifications of the cylinder head were unchanged, from engine number 091022 there were new valve guides and closing rockers. These allowed a valve guide seal to fit on top of the guide, similar to those on the valve spring engines. After engine number 091267 there was a new clutch housing, with longer clutch springs and six longer (5x16mm instead of 5x10mm) Allen screws. The earlier springs and screws were not interchangeable with this housing. All cylinder heads now had a manufacturing date stamp on them, but this indicated when the heads were cast, not assembled in engines or installed in chassis. This manufacturing date was often many months (or even years) earlier than the actual motorcycle production date.

Further ignition updates occurred after engine number 092220, the transducer assembly modified to allow the pickup air gaps to be set independently. The ignition plate spindle and spring were replaced and the ignition pickups screwed into two additional plates positioned behind the main plate. The 5mm pickup screws were slightly longer (14mm instead of 10mm) and

The kick-start 900 engine was essentially unchanged for 1981. (Courtesy Ducati Motor)

the 6mm main plate fixing screws slightly shorter (20mm instead of 30mm). This modification also required an alteration inside the clutch cover so the clutch covers were interchangeable. With the new set-up came a revised four-step ignition curve. The spark advance was now 6 degrees to 900rpm; 16-18 degrees at 1800rpm; 28 degrees at 2800rpm; and maximum advance of 32 degrees at 4000rpm. Two types of spark plug caps were still fitted, although most 1981 engines had the electrical suppressed type instead of KLG.

Both Dell'Orto PHF 32C and PHM 40B carburettors were fitted to the 1981 900 Super Sport. The PHM 40Bs had slightly different jetting to the earlier PHM 40A and were often fitted with shorter aluminium bell mouths. The PHM 40Bs also featured larger (22mm) float bowl nuts and a choke mechanism similar to that on the PHF 32C. The white plastic choke lever was mounted on a bracket on the left rear downtube. Air filters were retained with the 32mm carburettors. The standard exhaust system included Silentium mufflers (although Contis were still an option), single-walled exhaust header pipes, and chrome-plated steel exhaust header nuts that were now chrome-plated steel. The front nut was often lock wired.

There were new fairing decals for 1981, with no 'DESMO' on the lowers. (Courtesy Ducati Motor)

The updated seat for the 1981 Super Sport incorporated much more generous padding. (Courtesy Ducati Motor)

Frame numbers for the 1981 900 Super Sport continued the previous DM860SS number sequence, from around 090100. Because the 900 MHR shared engine numbers there was now little correlation between 900 Super Sport engine and frame numbers. The engine number was often considerably higher than the frame number after 1980. The black-painted frame was basically unchanged, carrying the Silentium muffler homologation plate.

Most of the changes for 1981 were to the bodywork. The silver paint was intentionally designed to replicate the earlier 900 Super Sport, but with new decals for the 18-litre steel fuel tank, half fairing, dual seat and side covers. The tank and side cover decals were blue. Generally there was a lockable fuel filler cap, and grey plastic Paioli fuel taps as on the last 1980 900 Super Sports. The fuel line was still green plastic, and the taps operated independently, without a junction underneath the tank. There were also new ABS mudguards, the front initially shaped as before but without any stripes. The dual seat was a completely different design with a removable (and lockable) seat pad. The seat sat low over the rear subframe with a cut-out over the top shock absorber mount. The fairing also featured a larger headlight opening with new rubber seal, and on early examples didn't include a cross brace or 'DESMO' decals.

The Marzocchi suspension was the same as for 1980, with a black-painted fork and 310mm shock absorbers. During the year some examples were fitted with the front fork of the 1981 900 MHR. Still with black-painted fork legs, the upper plug was now a 30mm hex and the fork legs included a different four-bolt mudguard mount. Most of these forks also had new top triple clamps, but there was some inconsistency and a mixture of fork types on some bikes.

Two types of gold-painted FPS wheel were fitted to the 1981 Super Sport, one with a four-bolt disc attachment and the other with a six-bolt attachment. As on the 900 MHR (and 900 SSD), the six-bolt type required new drilled discs with aluminium carriers. Most 1981 Super Sports had the six-bolt type. The tyres were generally Michelin M45 and initially the Brembo brake calipers 'Goldline' as in 1980. From frame number 090602 the brake calipers were black 08 series standardised with the rest of the bevel-drive line-up. These had a single bleed nipple and plastic pad covers and were interchangeable with the 'Goldline'. The chain guard was still stainless steel on the 1981 Super Sports. On the 1981 900 Super

Right: The 1981 Super Sport initially featured 'Goldline' Brembo brake calipers.

Below right: The 1981 dual seat base had a cutout to clear the rear shock absorber mount. (Courtesy Ducati Motor)

Sport the steel folding footpegs and chrome-plated steel foot levers were also as for 1980.

The electrical system and controls were carried over from the 1980 Super Sport. This included the Nippon Denso left handlebar switch, black Bosch horn, and 5-light CEV instrument panel. The headlight and taillight were also the same CEV and the wiring included the same small Bosch fuse box. This now featured a clip-on plastic cover without a retaining screw. While most 1981 Super Sports had Veglia instruments, Smiths were still fitted on occasion (particularly on US examples). Other ancillary components were also shared with 1980, including the Pantah-style clutch cable adjuster, black clutch lever and black plastic Verlicchi throttle.

The view from the cockpit was a familiar sight and included the older style CEV dashboard and switches. There was no fairing cross brace this year. (Courtesy Ducati Motor)

1981 900 Super Sport distinguishing features (from engine number DM860 090915-092919, frame number approx. DM860SS 090100-090694)

Manufacturing date stamp on cylinder heads
New Bosch ignition module connectors and pickups after engine number 090915
New valve guides and closing rockers after engine number 091022
New clutch housing with longer clutch springs after engine number 091267
New ignition pickup assembly after engine number 092220
Either Dell'Orto PHF 32C or PHM 40B carburettors fitted, both with a choke mechanism
Silentium mufflers standard and Contis an option
Black-painted frame
Silver-painted bodywork with new decals
Lockable fuel filler cap, grey plastic Paioli fuel taps, green fuel line
New ABS mudguards, the front without any stripes
New dual seat with removable seat pad and cut-out over the top shock absorber mount

Fairing with larger headlight opening with new rubber seal
Early fairings didn't include a cross brace or 'DESMO' decals
Some with a new front fork with a different four-bolt mudguard mount
Either four- or six-bolt FPS wheels
Brembo 'Goldline' brake calipers until frame number 090601
Black Brembo 08 brake calipers from frame number 090602
Stainless steel chain guard
Steel foot levers
Nippon Denso left handlebar switch
Bosch horn
5-light CEV instrument panel
CEV headlight and taillight
Most with Veglia instruments
Pantah-style clutch cable adjuster
Plastic Verlicchi throttle

900 Mike Hailwood Replica

The 900 Mike Hailwood Replica had been received very favourably and, for 1981, Ducati updated this model. With a focus on increasing production and improving practicality, most of the updates were cosmetic. This revised 900 MHR was displayed at the Bologna Show at the end of 1980, and went into production despite the tragic death of Mike Hailwood in March 1981 in a car accident. It became Ducati's most popular large displacement motorcycle, with 1500 produced in 1981.

Engine

The 1981 900 Mike Hailwood Replica continued to feature the kick-start 900 Super Sport engine, and shared the Super Sport number sequence. Engine numbers overlapped with the final 1980 900 MHR, some bikes with earlier engines if motorcycle production that day coincided with a batch of engines built sometime earlier. Most 1981 900 MHR engines had numbers after around 091400 where the 1980 version finished, and continued until 092919 when the engine received the six-dog gearbox. All the updates during the year were shared with the 900 Super Sport, and included updated ignition module connectors and pickups, alternator rotor, new valve guides and closing rockers, new clutch housing, and manufacturing date stamped on the cylinder heads. While there was a choice of Silentium or Conti mufflers all 900 MHRs were fitted with Dell'Orto PHM 40B carburettors. These had a choke (with the lever mounted on the left of the instrument bracket), and a reducer at the intake manifold. The carburettors sometimes now had air cleaners, or open bell mouths. Most of these were a short open type held by a hose clamp but occasionally the earlier plastic bell mouths were fitted.

Despite the larger seat the 900 Super Sport still presented a narrow rear profile. (Courtesy Ducati Motor)

Chassis

Frame numbers began at around 900750 for the updated 1981 900 MHR, but there was now a new frame designation and homologation number. The prefix was now DM900R, with a DGM 50235 OM homologation number. Most 900 MHRs also had a silencer homologation plate underneath the right-hand side cover with the homologation number DM 900 R E3 9R-37617.

The red-painted Super Sport-derived frame was basically unchanged but for small details. This included side cover screw attachments and folding lifting handle on the left. The rider's footpeg mount was changed so that it slotted into a clamped hole without a thread but the steel levers were unchanged. The main update for 1981 was a two-piece fairing, with a removable lower section. This lower section now included large white 'DUCATI' decals on the side. The fairing plexiglass was unchanged, still retained by nine 4x20mm screws. The 24-litre steel fuel tank was unchanged, although the chrome-plated fuel filler cap was now lockable. A new seat unit (produced by Selle NISA, Forli) and side covers now hid the rear carburettor and battery. There were still two small green flashes on the rear of the fibreglass solo seat cover, and the seat covering was as for 1980. The mudguards were now red ABS, a similar shape to before, but some 1981 MHRs were fitted with a black plastic front mudguard, similar to that of the 500 SL Pantah.

A slightly updated 38mm Marzocchi fork was fitted to the 900 MHR for 1981. Still with black-painted fork legs and a 140mm stroke, the upper plug was changed to accept a 30mm hex wrench, and there was a new 231mm damper rod. Most of these forks also had new top triple clamps and fork legs with different front mudguard mounts, while the fork cups retained a chrome ring. The 330mm Marzocchi shock absorbers were unchanged.

All 900 MHRs now had gold-painted aluminium FPS wheels with a six-bolt attachment for the front discs. From frame number 901301 black Brembo 08 brake calipers replaced the 'Goldline' brake calipers. While the rubber brake

Bodywork updates for the 1981 900 MHR included a two-piece fairing and side covers to hide the battery and rear carburettor. (Courtesy Ducati Motor)

105

The 900 MHR kick-start engine was shared with the Super Sport, but MHRs had 40mm carburettors. This early specification 1981 prototype doesn't feature the side covers, but does include the two-piece fairing. (Courtesy Ducati Motor)

Below left: Most 1981 900 MHRs had a red front mudguard, but only the earliest examples featured 'Goldline' Brembo brake calipers. (Courtesy Ducati Motor)

Below right: Conti mufflers were still fitted to many 1981 900 MHRs. (Courtesy Ducati Motor)

hoses were unchanged, the rear brake line now included a wire guide to prevent the line fouling the rear wheel. There was no change to the electrical system, or instrumentation, from the 1980 version, although a specific miles per hour speedometer was no longer specified. US versions came with an engine stop switch on the left handlebar, and there was a new clutch cable adjuster. Most ancillary components were shared with the 900 Super Sport and 600 SL Pantah.

1981 900 Mike Hailwood Replica distinguishing features (from engine number approx. DM860 091400-092919, frame number DM900R 900751-901800 approx.)

Engines shared with 900 Super Sport with the same updates

New Bosch ignition module connectors and pickups after engine number 090915

New valve guides and closing rockers after engine number 091022

New clutch housing with longer clutch springs after engine number 091267

New ignition pickup assembly after engine number 092220

Dell'Orto PHM 40B carburettors with choke and intake reducer

Carburettors with air cleaners or open bell mouths

Silentium or Conti mufflers

Frame with DM900R designation, side cover screw attachments, folding lifting handle, new footpeg mount

Two-piece fairing with large white 'DUCATI' side decals on the side

Lockable fuel filler cap

New Selle NISA seat and side covers

Red ABS mudguards but some with a black plastic front mudguard

New 38mm Marzocchi fork with 30mm upper plug, new top triple clamps and different front mudguard mounts

Gold-painted aluminium FPS wheels with a six-bolt disc attachment

From frame number 901301 black Brembo 08 brake calipers

Rear brake line now included a wire guide

Racing the 900 Super Sport during 1981

The 1980 Barcelona endurance race result and Francini's Italian TT1 Championship proved the venerable 900 bevel-drive was still a force to be reckoned with and encouraged the factory to maintain development. Two official machines were prepared for the 1981 Barcelona 24-hour race, both modified square-case 900 Super Sports. The frame was stock, with a round-section swingarm, while the engines displaced 950cc and featured a two-into-one exhaust system. The previous year's winners, Mallol and Tejedo, rode one machine, and Benjamin Grau and Enrique de Juan the other. Grau and de Juan covered 771 laps to take second place, but Mallol and Tejedo were slowed by three punctures caused by breakages of their Campagnolo wheels. By 1981 the emerging Superbike class had overtaken TT Formula 1 and NCR prepared a 947cc 900 SS-based Superbike for Sauro Pazzaglia in the Italian series. This machine featured 90mm pistons, 44 and 38mm valves, a special two-into-one exhaust system, a half fairing, and a round-section swing arm.

Also new for 1981 was the Battle of the Twins racing series. After a trial race in October 1980, the 11-race series began at Daytona in March 1981. The GP class was dominated by Jimmy Adamo on the Reno Leoni-tuned Ducati. His square-case 860 produced 96-98 horsepower at 9000rpm, the 80-degree cylinder heads featured 44 and 39mm valves, 10.8:1 compression, and the rubber-mounted carburettors were 41mm Malossi. The battery-powered Bosch ignition was run as total loss, and Leoni undercut the gears three degrees and radiused the dogs to eliminate the problem of the gears disengaging. Other modifications included longer (leading axle 750 GT) Marzocchi fork tubes, Moto Guzzi Le Mans 300mm disc rotors, and a wider swingarm to accommodate the largest rear slick tyre available. Although the increased drag of the larger rear tyre reduced the top speed on the banking from 157mph to 149mph, Adamo won the inaugural Daytona BOTT race at 101.106mph. Richard Schlachter was second on the George Vincensi round-case racer and Adamo went on to win the Battle of The Twins GP series in 1981.

Sauro Pazzaglia rode an NCR-prepared 947cc racer in the 1981 Italian Superbike series. (Courtesy Ducati Motor)

900 Sport Desmo 'Darmah'

The 900 SD received a few updates for 1981 and there were a few more inconsistencies in specification. Now only offered in black and gold, apart from the kick-start assembly, the electric start engine was standardised with the Super Sport, and the frame with the 900 SSD. Production was increased to 683 this year, and of these 376 went to Australia.

Engine

Engine numbers for 1981 coincided with new Bosch ignition transducers and terminal blocks. The terminal blocks were shared with the Pantah and fitted after engine number 905168. Further updates occurred shortly afterwards. From engine number 905553, there was a new steel clutch drum with new clutch springs and longer (5x16mm) Allen fasteners. Also from this engine number were new valve guide seals, the single inner O-ring replaced by an outer seal. The closing rockers were modified to allow for clearance around the new valve guide seal. The next update was after engine number 906029. The ignition pickup mounting was changed to allow for the adjustment of individual air gaps and saw a new transducer plate, spindle, and four fastening screws. Also for 1981 the manufacturing date was stamped on the cylinder heads.

Chassis

The 1981 frame designation was still DM900SD, with the DGM 19139 OM homologation number, numbers beginning at 951262. They went through until 952250, but as always there was some overlap between engine and frame numbers. While all 900 SDs were black and gold this year, there was

By 1981 the 900 SD was using many 900 SSD components, such as FPS wheels with six-bolt drilled discs. Colours were black and gold only this year. (Courtesy Two Wheels)

inconsistency in the type of Paioli fuel tap fitted. Some fuel taps were the grey plastic type, and others with a black plastic coated lever without a plastic chamber. The first 900 SDs for the 1981 model year were fitted with gold FPS wheels with 6-bolt drilled discs with aluminium carriers. These wheels were fitted between frame number 951261 and 951376, and after that featured a four-bolt disc. Also after frame number 951376 two 8mm dowels were fitted to the FPS cush drive flange. The tyres were either Pirelli Phantom or Michelin M45.

During 1981 production of the 900 SSD ceased and after frame number 951821 some SSD components were used on the 900 SD. There was obviously an oversupply of 900 SSD frames as they were now used on the 900 SD. The 900 SSD frame included the revised rear master cylinder mount and there was a new right-hand side cover. This had a diagonal cut at the rear for the brake line and no longer had three round holes. The black plastic rear mudguard was blanked off where the

earlier brake line went. Also new for the 900 SD with the SSD frame was a straight rear brake rod with a balljoint linkage instead of the clevis type. Other SSD frame features included the rear-set footpeg mounts but sometimes the front fairing mount on the steering head. The Bosch 180mm headlight was also the 900 SSD type.

Other updates that occurred after the implementation of the 900 SSD frame included new rear shock absorbers, now sometimes oleo-pneumatic Marzocchi with black springs and non-finned, silver-painted reservoirs. As an alternative to the Marzocchi shocks, Paioli shock absorbers were also specified but rarely fitted as standard equipment. Some of the Marzocchi fork legs were painted black and had revised castings for the four-bolt front mudguard attachment. There was a yellow 'Marzocchi' decal on the lower left fork leg, and a revised threaded spring retaining plugs in the top of the fork tubes. These required a 30mm hexagon spanner for removal instead of the

1981 900 SD 'Darmah' distinguishing features (from engine number DM860 905168-906305, frame number DM900SD 951261-952250)

New ignition terminal blocks after engine number 905168

From engine number 905553 new clutch drum and clutch springs

From engine number 905553 new valve guide seals

From engine number 906029 new ignition pickup mounting

Colours of black and gold

6-bolt FPS wheels between frame number 951261 and 951376

After frame number 951376 two 8mm dowels were fitted to the cush drive

After frame number 951821 900 SSD frame used with revised rear master cylinder mount and new right-hand side cover

After frame number 951821 straight rear brake rod with a balljoint linkage

After frame number 951821 some frames with rear-set footpeg mounts and front fairing mount

After frame number 951821 900 SSD Bosch headlight

After frame number 951821 some with new rear shock absorbers

After frame number 951821 some with black Marzocchi fork legs and new front mudguard attachment

After frame number 951821 most 6-bolt FPS wheels and drilled discs

Occasionally Speedline wheels fitted

Brembo brake calipers still twin bleeder

earlier 12mm Allen wrench. The rear brake caliper support plate still had three round holes.

Along with the 900 SSD frame was inconsistency in wheel and brake type. Most 900 SDs after frame number 951821 were also fitted with 900 SSD FPS wheels with six-bolt drilled discs, but there were still some with four-bolt FPS wheels and either drilled or solid discs. Occasionally Speedline wheels also appeared on the 900 SD during 1981, while the Brembo brake calipers remained the twin bleeder type that featured on the 900 SD since 1977.

900 Super Sport Desmo 'Darmah'

By 1981 the 900 SSD was being phased out, although a small number (126) were built as Australian specification this year. All of these remained at the factory as export records don't show any 900 SSDs sent to Australia in 1981. Engine and frame numbers were still shared with the 900 SD, engine numbers beginning at 905168 and frame numbers at DM900SD 951261. Frame numbers finished at 951820, although it is possible some 900 SSDs were built after this number cut-off. 900 SSD engine numbers finished sometime before 906029 (around 905850) and didn't include the new ignition pickup mounts. All the other 1981 900 SD engine updates were also incorporated on the 900 SSD. The frame and chassis components were unchanged from 1980, except from frame number 951376 the rear FPS wheel had two 8mm dowels to maintain the alignment of the cush drive flange with the hub 900 SSDs built in 1981 were stockpiled and sold into 1982, 1983 and even 1984. Ostensibly the 900 SSD for 1981 was unchanged from 1980.

CHAPTER NINE

1982 – 900 SS, 900 MHR, 900 SD

The 1982 900 Super Sport was ostensibly identical to the 1981 version. The lower fairing mostly had 'DESMO' decals this year.

Ducati was looking healthy by the end of 1981. The rationalisation of updated models introduced during 1981 resulted in significantly increased motorcycle production.

This led Ducati to approach 1982 positively, with its largest official display at the Milan Show since 1973. New colours featured for nearly all models. The 900 MHR was restyled, now all red with green

and white stripes, black Silentium mufflers, black FPS wheels with red rims, and black 600 SL-type front mudguard. Also appearing was a new 900 SD with a fairing and panniers. Although neither of these display models entered production in this form they indicated that the VM management was still committed to motorcycles and the continued development of the bevel-drive models. Undoubtedly this commitment was enhanced by the appointment of Cosimo Calcagnile as general manager. Calcagnile was unlike previous VM appointments as he'd had a longer association with Ducati, joining the company in 1956 at the age of 22. He was commercial director for 25 years prior to becoming general manager. Motorcycle production during 1982 was down on 1981, but still healthy, with 5665 motorcycles built. Of these, 2850 were 900 bevel-twins. 1983 model 900 S2s built after September are also included in this figure.

900 Super Sport

Although the basic style of the 900 Super Sport was unchanged for 1982, there were some important updates. The engines for 1982 started at number DM860 092920, and the frames at DM860SS 090695, but as engines were still built earlier and stacked in racks prior to assembly in frames, there was some overlap in engine and frame numbers. As engines were shared with the 900 MHR, engine numbers continued to diverge from frame numbers. Engine numbers for the 900 Super Sport finished around 094600 but this number sequence continued for the kick-start 900 MHR and later 900 S2.

Engine

The most significant engine update for 1982 was the replacement of the previous 6-dog gearbox with a new 3-dog type. This update occurred after engine number 092920 and was an improvement that featured on racing engines since 1978. The dogs on the gears were much longer and, while gear selection wasn't as crisp, the 3-dog gears were stronger and less likely to jump out of engagement. There were also now two oil seal retaining circlips, instead of one, inside the output shaft. At the same time the two 32- and 70-tooth primary drive gears and clutch housing were updated. These were previously fitted independently but the new gears came as a matched set. From engine number 094150 the

aluminium/bronze valve seats were replaced by a cast-iron type. At this time there were also two sizes of con-rod small-end bushes fitted at the factory. Until this time only a 23mm outer diameter bush was fitted but now there were two sizes of con-rod bush (23.00mm and 23.30mm). This was possibly due to a new supplier of forged con-rods and a result of inaccurate con-rod machining. During 1982 the 10mm cylinder head nuts with curved washer and 16mm head were replaced by a 10x10mm nut (with 17mm head) and flat 10.5mm washer. The kick-start remained unchanged but for a revised special 8x30mm lever retaining screw. Many 1982 900 Super Sports were fitted with Dell'Orto PHM 40B carburettors with short aluminium bell mouths, and Silentium mufflers. The choke lever was still on the left at the rear of the fuel tank.

Chassis

The black-painted 900 Super Sport frame was initially unchanged from 1981, with frame numbers beginning at 090695 and finishing around 091800 for 1982. Most 1982 frames included a fold out

The seat base was new for 1982, no longer cut out over the top snock absorber mount.

Most 1982 900 Super Sports had six-bolt discs, and the front fork with revised mudguard mounting lugs.

handle on the left like the 900 Mike Hailwood Replica, but this was an inconsistent feature. Most 1982 900 Super Sports also had a silencer homologation plate with a new stamp face. The rear seat unit was new after number 090695, not sitting as low, and clearing the shock absorber without a cut-out. While the fairing was unchanged, a top aluminium cross brace (as on the 900 MHR) was fitted to most 1982 900 Super Sports and there were now 'DESMO' decals on each side. Towards the end of the production run the front mudguard was mostly an angular ABS 600 SL Pantah type, and the side covers solid ABS without aluminium mesh. There were many inconsistencies in specification towards the end of the production run, some even with 1978 blue and silver steel fuel tanks and front mudguards with early stripes. Most 1982 Super Sports featured the stainless steel chain guard of earlier Super Sports, but some later examples had a black chain guard. Minor updates introduced during the year included aluminium foot levers with 'DUCATI' castings and removable ends. The other chassis components were as before; including a later Marzocchi fork with revised mudguard mounts, and gold FPS wheels with six-bolt discs. Unlike the 1982 900 MHR the fork cups retained a chrome ring.

Production of the 1982 900 Super Sport was concentrated early in the 1982 model year (after September 1981) and only 335 were built in 1982. Sales were almost at a standstill, and many of these

Also new for 1982 was a fairing top brace. The top triple clamp and fork tube nuts were also updated during the year. This US specification example also has Smiths instruments.

1982 900 Super Sport distinguishing features (from engine number DM860 09292C-094600 approx., frame number DM860SS 090695-091800 approx.)

Three-dog gearbox after engine number 092920
New primary drive gears and clutch housing
Cast-iron valve seats after engine number 094150
10x10mm cylinder head nuts with flat 10.5mm washers
New kick-start lever retaining screw
Many with Dell'Orto PHM 40B carburettors with short bell mouths
Most frames included a fold out handle on the left

New silencer homologation plate
New seat unit clearing the shock absorber without a cut-out
Fairing with aluminium cross brace and "DESMO" decals
Front mudguard was mostly an angular ABS type
Solid side covers without aluminium mesh
Some with 1978 fuel tanks and front mudguards
Some with a black chain guard
Aluminium foot levers introduced during the year

final Super Sports (186) were sold in Australia at discount prices. By early 1982 Ducati already had plans for a Super Sport replacement, the 900 S2 for 1983. After eight years the 900 Super Sport finally came to an end. 6103 were produced, and it would live on as one of Ducati's greatest ever production models. More than any other model the 900 Super Sport exemplified the finest attributes of the Ducati motorcycle of the late 1970s. Providing charisma, balance, fine handling, and excellent power, this is the machine that epitomises Ducatis of this era. In all incarnations the 900 Super Sport was one of the outstanding sporting motorcycles of all time.

900 Mike Hailwood Replica

Although an updated 900 MHR was presented at the 1981 Milan Show the production MHR continued for 1982 with only minor updates. This year most bevel-twin production was centred on the 900 MHR, with 1549 produced. Some of these were similar 1983 models produced after September. The kick-start engine was still shared with the 900 Super Sport, with the same engine number sequence (092920-094600 approx.). 1982 modifications included the 3-dog gearbox (after engine number 092920), two sizes of small-end con-rod bush, cast-iron valve seats (after engine number 094150), new cylinder head nuts and washers, and new kick-start lever retaining screw. All 1982 90 MHRs were fitted with Dell'Orto PHM 40B carburettors, with short aluminium bell mouths but some also came with air cleaners. The choke lever was attached on the left, next to the headlamp. Silentium mufflers were mostly fitted as standard equipment for 1982.

900 MHR frame numbers for 1982 continued from approximately DM900R 901800 to 903300. To improve ground clearance the Marzocchi front fork was modified this year, with a longer fork tube (590mm instead of 580mm), a shorter damper rod (221mm instead of 231mm), and longer damper rod retaining bolts (12x40mm instead of 12x35mm). The fork travel was reduced to 130mm, and the fork oil capacity increased to 250cc. The reduced travel fork was complemented by reduced travel Marzocchi shock absorbers. Still 330mm in length, the stroke was 80mm (instead of 90mm).

The seat pad retaining system was changed for 1982, with a front slide-on fixing plate on the seat base instead of a pin and rubber grommet. The front fairing supports were now painted red (instead of chrome-plated). Other new features introduced during 1982 included aluminium foot

1982 900 Mike Hailwood Replica distinguishing features (from engine number approx. DM860 092920-094600, frame number approx. DM900R 901800-903300)

Three-dog gearbox after engine number 092920
New primary drive gears and clutch housing
Cast-iron valve seats after engine number 094150
10x10mm cylinder head nuts with flat 10.5mm washers
New kick-start lever retaining screw
Many with Dell'Orto PHM 40B carburettors with short bell mouths
Marzocchi front fork with 590mm tubes and 221mm damper rod

80mm stroke Marzocchi shock absorbers
New seat pad retaining system
Red-painted front fairing supports
Aluminium foot levers introduced during the year
Larger red ABS front mudguard
Red chain guard
Two centre stand return springs

Most updates to the 1982 MHR were to the engine and suspension, so it looked similar to the 1981 version.

The 900 MHR was Ducati's most popular model during 1982. This example (engine 093001, frame 902084) is very representative of this year.

levers with screw ends and 'DUCATI' pressings, and a larger red ABS front mudguard. The chain guard was sometimes red-painted steel, and the centre stand had two return springs instead of one. The decals were unchanged (including the seat flashes), and, visually, there was little to differentiate the 1982 900 MHR from the 1981 version.

Racing the 900 during 1982

Although Ducati saw its racing programme increasingly based on the new-generation Pantah, a 900 TT1/Coupe d'Endurance machine was displayed at the 1981 Bologna Show for the 1982 racing season. This factory bike was the final official bevel-drive racer and featured a square-case engine with an electric start. It was raced in some endurance events during 1982 by Carlo Perugini and Mauro Ricci, and in the Italian TT1 series by Radicchio and Lisi. The 900 was only moderately successful this year, its most impressive finish on 17-18 July in the Montjuich 8-Hour race. Here Carlos Cardus, Benjamin Grau

and Enrique de Juan came fourth. It was the 900 Ducati's final fling in endurance racing, but, considering the design was 12 years old, it was an impressive achievement.

Adamo's 900 bevel-twin continued to dominate the US Battle of the Twins in 1982, his Leoni-built 989cc (with 92mm pistons) machine now producing nearly 100 horsepower at 9000rpm. The success of Battle of the Twins in America soon saw it established in the UK and Europe, Dave Railton setting the pace on his 950 bevel-twin during 1982.

900 Sport Desmo 'Darmah'

At the Milan Show at the end of 1981, two slightly restyled 900 SDs were displayed for 1982. One had an optional fairing, rack and panniers that didn't become available, but there were new colours for 1982. These included light blue, light red, light burgundy, or light bronze-gray, with subtle striping. The colour of the stripes and decals varied with gold on red bikes and silver with bronze or blue. Some of the bronze versions also had red highlighting, so

Radicchio rode the electric start 900 SS racer in the 1982 Italian TT1 series. This was the final factory bevel-drive racer. (Courtesy Ducati Motor)

117

there was some inconsistency in decals this year. Most 1982 model year 900 SDs were produced in the latter part of 1981 in the traditional black and gold, and only 317 900 SDs were manufactured during 1982 in the new colours. Although the 900 SD was an extremely successful model, lasting five years with minimal development, it wasn't the most profitable. The desmodromic engine was identical in specification to the more expensive 900 Super Sport and Mike Hailwood Replica, but the 900 SD offered an electric start and complete Nippon Denso equipment. Faced with declining sales, 1982 would be the 900 SD's final official year of production.

Engine numbers for 1982 began at DM860 906306 when the three-dog gearbox replaced the six-dog type. Along with the new gearbox came primary gears in matched sets, rather than as individual gears. After engine number 906479 cast-iron valve seats replaced the bronze seats and the gearbox drum fixing screw was loctited, to prevent it from loosening prematurely. The final 900 SD engine was around 907000.

Production for 1982 began during 1981, from frame number DM900SD 952251, continuing until approximately 953200. The most noticeable update was the replacement of the swingarm with a 900 Super Sport type with Seeley chain adjusters and aluminium axle support plates. This update

was implemented to overcome the limitations to the adjustment purely with the eccentric. This provided only limited adjustment, but also altered the relationship between the swingarm pivot and countershaft sprocket. The new swingarm was directly interchangeable with the earlier 900 SD type (but not the 900 Super Sport) but required a new rear wheel, axle and spacers. The eccentric adjustment at the swingarm pivot was retained and frames were still the 900 SSD type. Some had rear set mounts and others were without, while some had the steering head frame supports while others didn't. With the new swingarm came a slightly redesigned silencer homologation plate, still mounted in the same position with the same numbers. Also from frame number 952251 the twin bleed nipple Brembo brake calipers were standardised with a single bleed nipple type shared with the 900 Super Sport and MHR.

Towards the end of production there was some inconsistency in the specification of wheels, brakes, and rear shock absorbers as existing stock was utilised. Most 900 SDs had FPS wheels with six-bolt discs, but some were also fitted with four-bolt drilled discs. There was also some inconsistency in the type of brake caliper, with twin bleed calipers sometimes fitted, along with the earlier rear brake caliper support bracket. The rear shock absorbers were mostly the later type

This red 900 SD was shown at the 1981 Bologna Show and, while the colour scheme was retained for 1982, the touring equipment didn't become available. (Courtesy Ducati Motor)

Marzocchi remote reservoir, but some examples had the earlier, finned Marzocchi shock absorbers. The Marzocchi fork still featured black fork legs but sometimes there was no chrome ring on the cups. Other small updates included a reshaped rear brake rod, lockable fuel cap, and sometimes the black ABS front mudguard of the Pantah. Some later 900 SDs also had non-sequential frame numbers and the earlier DGM 13715 OM frame homologation number.

Although official 900 SD production ceased during 1982 many machines and spare parts remained in storage at the factory. In 1983 109 900 SDs were shipped to Australia and some of these were built several years earlier. At least one example had a 1984 electric start 900 MHR engine in a 1979 chassis (with a 1979 frame number but with later Oscam wheels) and a 10/84 build date. With a total of 5598 examples produced between 1977 and 1982 the 900 SD was one of the more numerous bevel-twins but hasn't earned the appreciation it really warrants.

One of the most attractive 900 SDs was the blue (with silver decals) version of 1982.
(Courtesy Ducati Motor)

1982 900 SD 'Darmah' distinguishing features (from engine number DM860 906306-907000 approx., frame number DM900SD 952251-953200 approx.)

Three-dog gearbox from engine number 906306

Primary gears in matched sets

Cast-iron valve seats from engine number 906479

From frame number 952251 swingarm with 900 SS chain adjusters

Frame still the 900 SSD type, most with rear set mounts and steering head support

From frame number 952251 single bleed nipple Brembo brake calipers

Colours of either black and gold, bronze, or blue (with new stripes)

Most with six-bolt discs but some were with 4-bolt drilled discs

Some with twin bleed calipers and earlier rear brake caliper support bracket

Either early or later Marzocchi remote reservoir shock absorbers

Marzocchi fork with black fork legs and sometimes without chrome rings

Reshaped rear brake rod

Lockable fuel cap

Some with non-sequential frame numbers and DGM 13715 OM homologation

CHAPTER TEN

1983 – 900 S2, 900 MHR

By mid-1982 Ducati had reached a crossroads and was in a dilemma as to how to proceed with updating its bevel-drive range. Although the Pantah was seen as the key to the future, Ducati's chief engineer Fabio Taglioni was still enthusiastic to retain the bevel-drive twin as a large capacity range leader. But he realised the days of the kick-start only Super Sport were numbered, and demand for the long-running 900 SD 'Darmah' virtually non-existent. Fabio Taglioni was already working on a new version, the 'Mille', but this was still some time away and Ducati needed an updated model in the interim. As the existing 900 twins were still very much 1970s motorcycles Ducati saw the need to incorporate some fashionable features to expand the 900's appeal. The result was the 900 S2, a 900 Super Sport replacement incorporating features of the 900 SD 'Darmah' and 600 SL Pantah. The the 900 S2 was first presented in July 1982, with an official press release in September 1982 at Imola. It went into production in September 1982 as a 1983 model, and 649 were produced before the end of the year. The only other bevel-twin in the line-up for 1983 was the 900 Mike Hailwood Replica, this continuing as a kick-start only model with minimal changes from 1982. Production was down for 1983, to 3909 motorcycles, and 687 of these were electric start 900 MHRs for the 1984 model year. 1983 represented the beginning of the end for the venerable bevel-drive twin as the cost of production overtook its meagre profits.

Ducati was a victim of a worldwide slump in motorcycle sales, one that also hit the other niche Italian manufacturers hard. Consequently, it wasn't only Ducati that had difficulty adapting its aging existing designs to an increasingly fashion-driven market. Laverda, Moto Guzzi, and Benelli were in a similar predicament and not all these companies managed to weather the storm. Although, as a government-controlled company, Ducati was still better positioned to survive than smaller companies like Laverda, by 1983 the VM Group was looking for a way out from motorcycle manufacture. VM was also suffering a downturn in the demand for automotive diesel engines and, early in 1983 began talks with Cagiva in Varese to provide engines for a range of Cagiva motorcycles. This initially called for Ducati to supply 6000 engines in 1984, 10,000 in 1985, and 14,000 in 1986. Cagiva also wanted Taglioni to complete the development of his V4 but as this development was in its infancy the idea of a V4 appearing soon was optimistic. The agreement with Cagiva was announced on June 1 1983.

900 S2

With a significant supply of new 900 Super Sports awaiting delivery at the factory during 1982, 900 SS production slowly ground to a halt. It was obvious to Ducati's management that the 900 Super Sport could no longer continue in its present form, and early in 1982 a decision was made to revamp it. Ostensibly this update was intended to broaden the appeal of Ducati's once staple sporting model, at the same time launching it into the 1980s with

more modern styling. In retrospect this wasn't an inspired transformation and the 900 S2 failed to win a new band of devotees. However, while not one of Ducati's success stories, the 900 S2 was still an excellent sporting motorcycle that continued the tradition of the Super Sport. 900 S2 production commenced in September 1982, in two forms; electric start and kick-start. The kick-start 900 S2 continued the engine number sequence of the 900 Super Sport, with the inevitable overlap, while the electric start 900 S2 continued the engine number sequence of the 900 SD. Although the frame was new, the number sequence continued that of the 900 Super Sport.

Kick-start engine

Kick-start 900 S2 engines overlapped with the 900 Mike Hailwood Replica, beginning around 094600 and ending at 095741 for the 900 S2 for the 1983 model year. Kick-start engines after this number were also fitted to the 900 MHR for 1983 and, although the kick-start engine was being phased out, there were still some updates. During 1983 the aluminium/bronze valve guides were replaced by cast-iron, and the ignition pickup plate modified again (following the previous update after engine number 092220). Although still retaining the additional two fixing plates, the 6mm nut was no longer attached to the plate but now fitted separately. The ignition coils were also changed from Bosch (with a separate Bosch resistor) to Motoplat (without a resistor), while the plastic spark plug caps all had a metal cover. These were designed to reduce electrical interference but were unreliable if the bike was ridden in the rain. To reduce noise, 25 rubber blocks were inserted between the fins of the cylinders and another 25 in the cylinder head fins.

The 900 S2 was designed to give the Super Sport line a new lease of life. (Courtesy Ducati Motor)

121

Except for those examples destined for France 900 S2s were fitted with Dell'Orto PHM 40B carburettors. For France the carburettors were Dell'Orto PHF 32A. All 900 S2s had air cleaners with individual metal air boxes and an oil breather tank under the seat. Unlike the 900 Super Sport (but as on the 900 SD) the rear intake manifold was now the same as the front to allow the carburettor to clear the larger battery on the electric start model. Although the kick-start 900 S2 featured the usual smaller 12Ah battery of the Super Sport it also featured a front intake manifold on the rear cylinder. The new exhaust system featured double-walled header pipes with the left header pipe now angled closer to the engine to improve ground clearance. The standard mufflers were Silentium (with a kick-start indent on the right-hand side), or optional Conti mufflers. These had more rearward brackets than those on the Super Sport as the passenger footpegs were further back on the S2 frame. Fewer kick-start 900 S2s were built than electric start, with 173 built in 1982 (as 1983 models) and a further 180 during 1983. Some of these were 1984 models built after September 1983.

Electric start engine

Most 900 S2s were built as electric start versions,

476 in 1982 as 1983 models and 202 in 1983. The engine number sequence continued where the 900 SD left off, beginning around DM860 907000, and continuing to 907428 for the 1983 model year. Engine updates were shared with the kick-start version, including a modified ignition plate, Motoplat ignition coils (without a separate resistor), rubber blocks inserted in the cylinder and head fins, and cast-iron valve guides. One update not immediately shared with the kick-start engines was a new Saprisa 200W, three-wire alternator and regulator. On electric start engines this was fitted after engine number 907231, but didn't feature on kick-start engines until the 1984 model year. The alternator stator differed on all electric start 900 S2 engines, shared with the Pantah and not the 900 MHR.

Chassis

Although the 900 S2 continued the 900 Super Sport number series and frame designation, the black-painted frame was quite different, and was an amalgam of the Super Sport and Darmah type, with a combination of features. The frame numbers for both kick- and electric start 900 S2 continued where the 900 Super Sport ended, around DM860SS 091800, and both types continued with the 900 SS frame homologation number (DGM 13715 OM) and silencer homologation plate (E3 9R-13716). While retaining the Super Sport 29½ degree steering head angle, with 145mm of trail, much of the construction was derived from the 860. The dimensions of the frame were significantly different to the 900 Super Sport, with the engine situated higher, the front downtubes flattened at the ends, and the rear downtubes bowed to provide room for the larger battery. The front mounting bolt was longer, at 285mm, and the right rear downtube was extensively hollowed and significantly weaker than this comparable section on the Super Sport frame. Both front downtubes also included bosses for a future fairing mount. Most centre stands were also the 900 Super Sport type, but during 1983 some of the feet were changed to the 900 SD-type.

In essence the 900 S2 was a styling, rather than functional, update of the 900 Super Sport. The 18-litre steel fuel tank was similar to the 900 Super Sport, but with a lockable black recessed fuel filler cap. This may have looked more modern than the earlier chrome-plated type, but allowed water into the tank leading to rust. The fuel taps were the usual gray Paioli with green plastic fuel lines. The ABS fairing and plexiglass screen was from the 600 SL Pantah and modified to provide clearance for the electric start motor on electric start versions. Early examples included a clear screen, but some later versions had a tinted screen. The eight 4mm threaded screen fasteners were also changed to plastic rivets.

For 1983 the front turn signals were flush mounted in the fairing. There was no top cross brace as a factory fitment but this was often added by distributors, as were mirrors. The lower fairing mounts were now separate brackets underneath the fuel tank and, initially, the fairing and side cover screws were chrome-plated with white washers. During 1983 these were changed to black with black washers. The seat and side covers were new, with a lockable seat pad similar to that on the 1981 900 Super Sport. 900 S2 colours for 1982 were bronze/grey, with orange 'DUCATI' decals on the tank, and red, orange, and yellow stripes. The black mudguards were constructed from ABS, the front including a guide for the speedometer cable, and the rear mudguard was in two pieces.

The 900 S2 received a new Marzocchi fork, similar to that on the 1983 900 MHR apart from a rear Brembo brake caliper mount. The fork legs were 590mm long, and the damper rod 221mm. There were new top inner fork seals and no chrome retaining rings on the dust seals. At the rear were new Marzocchi ET 85 shock absorbers, with black springs and a small yellow decal at the base. As on the 900 MHR shock absorber length was 330mm but the stroke was reduced to 75mm. The wheels for 1983 were still the gold-painted FPS, shod with Pirelli Phantom tyres. During the model year the rear sprocket attachment was updated, with the two locking plates removed. 8x40mm Allen bolts with nyloc nuts were now used instead of the previous hexagon head nuts.

The Brembo braking system was updated for the 900 S2. The three 280mm cast-iron disc rotors retained the six-bolt attachment but were a budget version without the separate alloy disc carriers. The drilling pattern was also only radial, not spiral. As the front brake calipers were now positioned behind the fork legs, there were new 485mm rubber brake hoses (without the metal connecting tubes) joining the brake caliper to the junction on the lower triple clamp. The rear brake setup was also new, the master cylinder with a remote reservoir mounted on a bracket near the battery, under the right-hand side cover. The rear master cylinder was operated directly from the lever (with a single 6mm balljoint), eliminating the rod and clevis joint of the 900 Super Sport. The aluminium levers and folding footpegs with rubbers were also new for the 900 S2, and the

chain guard was black. During 1983 the early-type foot lever rubbers were updated to match the passenger footpeg type.

Apart from the higher and forward-set clip-on handlebars, the controls and Nippon Denso instruments were shared with the 900 MHR. Electric start 900 S2s used a plastic Verlicchi dual cable throttle that incorporated the electric start and engine stop switch. On 1983 900 S2s the headlamp was the 170mm Bosch and the large rectangular taillight and rear turn signals CEV. The 900 S2 wasn't an entirely successful replacement for the 900 Super Sport as, during the transformation, it grew larger and gained weight. The provision of a larger battery tray compromised the frame design, as did the modifications to make the frame more economical to produce. With styling that didn't meet universal acclaim the 900 S2 struggled to achieve the following of the 900 Super Sport. Ultimately it survived as the basis for the next generation 900 Mike Hailwood Replica.

900 Mike Hailwood Replica

While the 900 S2 represented a new path for the Super Sport line, the 900 Mike Hailwood Replica continued essentially unchanged for 1983. All 1983 model MHRs were kick-start only, and 780 were produced. A few of these were built after September 1983 as 1984 models in the updated chassis. Engine numbers began around 094600, continuing to 096313. The engines were initially shared with the kick-start 900 S2, incorporating the same updates, but continued beyond 095741 of the 900 S2. Shared updates included cast-iron valve guides and modified ignition pickup plate, but the coils were still Bosch and the spark plug caps the earlier KLG rubber type. The 900 MHR also didn't receive noise-reducing rubber blocks between the cylinder and head fins. A new gear selector drum was fitted after engine number 095742, and there was a new Saprisa alternator rotor (and regulator) from engine number 096142.

The indicators were flush-mounted on the 1983 900 S2, and the headlamp Bosch.
(Courtesy Ducati Motor)

This was still 200W but not the same as that fitted to electric start engines.

The 1983 900 MHR was the final Ducati to use the 900 Super Sport frame and in this respect it differed from the 900 S2. Thus all the ancillary

components, including handlebars, footpegs, levers, and CEV headlight, taillight, and indicators were shared with the 1982 900 MHR and not the 900 S2 that was produced concurrently. The red-painted 900 MHR frame still used the DM900R designation and DGM 50235 OM homologation number, numbers beginning around 903300 until approximately 904600. Although the chassis was similar to the 1982 MHR there were some equipment updates. During 1983 the centre stand feet were reshaped as on the 900 SD, rather than the earlier 900 Super Sport. Most 1983 900 MHRs had the 900 S2 black ABS mudguards, the front mudguard including a guide for the speedometer

1983 900 S2 distinguishing features (from engine number approx DM860 094600-095741 kick-start; approx. DM860 907000-907428 electric start, frame number approx. DM860SS 091800-092600)

Cast-iron valve guides
Ignition pickup plate modified
Motoplat ignition coils
Rubber blocks inserted in cylinder and cylinder head fins
Dell'Orto PHM 40B carburettors with air cleaners
Rear intake manifold now the same as the front
Silentium or Conti mufflers with more rearward brackets
Saprisa alternator and regulator on electric start after engine number 907231
New black-painted frame with DM860SS homologation
Bronze/grey colours with orange tank decals and red, orange, and yellow stripes
Steel fuel tank with lockable black recessed fuel filler cap
Fairing similar to 600 SL Pantah with flush front turn signals
Fairing and side cover screws initially chrome plated then black
Later fairing screens tinted

Later fairing fasteners plastic rivets
New seat and side covers
Black ABS mudguards
New Marzocchi fork with rear Brembo brake caliper mount
New Marzocchi shock absorbers, with black springs
Gold-painted FPS wheels with Pirelli Phantom tyres
New six-bolt brake discs without alloy carriers and new drilling pattern
Remote reservoir rear master cylinder operated directly from the lever
New foot levers and folding footpegs
Higher and forward-set clip-on handlebars and 900 MHR controls and instruments
Electric start 900 S2s with plastic Verlicchi dual cable throttle
170mm Bosch headlamp
Large rectangular CEV taillight and rear turn signals

cable. Because of this chrome rings were not fitted to the front fork caps but otherwise the Marzocchi suspension was unchanged from the second 1982 type. The wheels were still gold-painted FPS with six-bolt discs but the 280mm drilled discs now featured larger cut outs where they met the carrier. Unlike the 900 S2 the drilling pattern was still spiral, and the front Brembo brake calipers remained forward mounted, with metal brake pipes joining the rubber brake lines. Other updates included a

red-painted steel chain guard and new seat decals, these now matching the tank. As the 1984 electric start version was already under development the 1983 900 MHR was an interim model. Most were destined for Japan that was emerging as Ducati's primary export market.

New seat decals set the 1983 900 MHR apart from the 1982 version. The black mudguards were also new. (Courtesy Nico Georgeoglou)

The front disc rotors featured larger holes where the discs met the alloy carrier. (Courtesy Nico Georgeoglou)

By 1983 all foot levers were aluminium. 1983 900 MHRs also retained the lifting lever on the left.
(Courtesy Nico Georgeoglou)

1983 900 Mike Hailwood Replica distinguishing features (from engine number approx. DM860 094600-096313, frame number approx. DM900R 903300-904600)

Cast-iron valve guides and modified ignition pickup plate
Bosch coils and KLG spark plug caps.
New gear selector drum after engine number 095742
No noise-reducing rubber blocks between the cylinder and head fins
Saprisa alternator rotor (and regulator) from engine number 096142
Red-painted frame with DM900R designation and DGM 50235 OM homologation

Most with black ABS mudguards
No chrome rings fitted to the front fork caps
FPS wheels with six-bolt discs
Drilled discs now featured larger cut outs
Red-painted steel chain guard
New seat decals
Earlier CEV headlight and taillight

CHAPTER ELEVEN

1984 – 900 S2, 900 MHR

The 1983 agreement with Cagiva initially allowed for Ducati to continue producing entire motorcycles until the end of 1984 whereupon, it would become an engine-only manufacturing plant. This dismal scenario resulted in only 1765 motorcycles being built during 1984, the lowest annual figure in Ducati's history. Apart from 32 600 SL Pantahs, all motorcycles built in 1984 were bevel-twins: the 900 S2 and 900 MHR. But, despite the agreement with Cagiva, there was still considerable uncertainty at Borgo Panigale. Development of the new Mille engine continued unabated, and, during 1984, the prospect of Ducati ending motorcycle production diminished as export markets requested the retention of the Ducati name on the motorcycles.

900 S2

At the end of 1983 two updated 900 S2s were displayed; one at the Milan Show and another at the Bologna Show. The first example was black with a red frame, with a belly pan with an orange 'DESMO' decal underneath the engine. The wheels were Oscam, with tubeless Michelin A48/M48 tyres, and the rear shock absorbers Marzocchi remote reservoir. The red-painted frame also featured some changes; notably a 900 SD-like centre stand. While the front turn signals were still flush-mounted in the fairing, the screen was tinted. The second example was red, with a red frame and red highlighted Oscam wheels. The front indicators were on stalks and the tank decals

replaced by badges. Both these versions of the 900 S2 foreshadowed how it would evolve during 1984. Unlike the 1983 900 S2 that was quite consistent in equipment, there were several different types during 1984. Nearly all 900 S2s were now electric start, though there were still a few with kick-start engines. These were the final kick-start engines produced by Ducati, and some included an added electric start. 900 S2 production for 1984 was only 205 examples, all of these electric start. The few kick-start 900 S2s for the 1984 model year were built towards the end of 1983. Another 1984 inconsistency saw many 900 S2s with 1984 build dates that were obviously built sometime earlier and stockpiled. The uncertainty caused by the Cagiva buyout undoubtedly affected the way motorcycles were produced at Borgo Panigale this year, as the small number of 900 S2s built are difficult to categorise.

Kick-start engine

As only a few kick-start 900 S2s were produced for the 1984 model year it is difficult to ascertain the exact engine number range. For the purposes of documentation it is convenient to establish the beginning of the 1984 version as those after engine number 095742, but most of these engines were installed in the 1983 900 MHR. It can be assumed that all kick-start engines were built during 1983, and the later examples fitted to chassis after September of that year. Engines after 095742 included a new gear selector drum, and after

number 096142 there was a Saprisa three-wire alternator and regulator. Although the rotor was the same as for the electric start alternator, the stator differed on kick-start engines.

The most significant update occurred after engine number 096314. New right-side crankcases included a spin-on oil filter with screw nipple, and an oil level sight glass. There was also an update for the oil supply line where it joined the alternator cover. Along with the previous oil filter and steel cover, several other components were removed. These included the rubber retaining block for the sump oil strainer and its 10mm locating screw, and the seal for the gear selector shaft behind the countershaft sprocket. The gear selector shaft no longer exited through the cases for the neutral indicator light switch, and this hole was now cast over, eliminating another potential oil leak. There was a new gearbox selector drum, lock washer, 4x15.5mm roller, and the neutral light switch was now located in the rear of the right crankcase. Due to the elimination of the internal rubber block there was a new crankcase oil strainer. The two upper crankcase retaining screws were now 8x55mm. Other updates included new gear location pins

for the lower straight cut timing gears, these now including a Seeger ring. There were sometimes difficulties in shimming the lower bevel gears on the square-case engine, and this modification was designed to improve this situation.

Basically the square-case 864cc engine was much as before. This included the same outer engine cases, cable-operated wet clutch, dipstick, and plug on the left crankcase half. Some of the final 1984 900 S2s featured kick-start engines, an electric start, and an electric kick-start engine number sequence. The final kick-start engine number was around 097200, some of these also featuring on the updated 1984 model 900 MHR.

Electric start engine

Electric start engine numbers for 1984 began at DM860 907429 when the new gear selector drum and retaining washer were installed. At some stage during 1984 the updated crankcases with the oil level glass and spin-on filter were also introduced on the electric start engines, but this was an inconsistent modification. Some

907600 series engines had these updates, but some 907700 series engines didn't. As on the kick-start version this update saw a new gear shift drum and neutral indicator light switch, new oil strainer, and timing gear retaining pins with a Seeger ring. Electric start 900 S2s also began to feature Silentium mufflers without a kick-start indent. Engine numbers for the electric start 900 S2 finished around 907900.

Frame

Although there wasn't really a definitive type of 1984 900 S2, they were all categorised by the new red-painted frame. Unlike the 1983 examples, frame numbers and the designation now differed between kick-start and electric start versions. The kick-start 900 S2 had a DM900SS prefix, with numbers continuing from approximately the previous 092600-series, while electric start versions used a DM900S2 designation. The DM900S2 also featured a new number sequence beginning at 095001, continuing to around 097000. To further complicate this mysterious change in numbering, kick-start frame numbers now began with an 'A' instead of '0', from around A92700, lasting until approximately A92800. There was also some overlap in numbers between the 'A' frame and the '0' type. Although identical in dimensions both kick-start and electric start frames had different frame homologation numbers, DM900SS continuing with the DGM 13715 OM homologation number and DM900S2 frames featuring a new DGM 51148 OM homologation number. Although the earliest 1983 frames carried the previous silencer homologation plate both frame types soon featured a new silencer homologation plate with two numbers (E3 9R-0040041 for Silentium and E3 9R 0440040 for Contis). Those few engines with a kick- and electric start mostly used the kick-start frame number sequence. The numbers sequences were remarkably confusing considering only 205 electric start 900 S2s were built in 1984, plus the few 1984 models made towards the end of 1983. Frame numbers seem to bear little correlation with actual production numbers with many numbers obviously omitted in the sequences.

The red-painted frame was basically the same as for 1983. Updates included a recess in

A period photo of a second series 1984 900 S2, the electric start engine with a spin-on oil filter. (Courtesy Two Wheels)

the left rear downtube as well as the right, further weakening the rear section of the frame, and a right-angle section above the left muffler bracket. This was to act as a lifting handle instead of the fold out lever. The centre stand feet were also the same as those on the 900 SD, with oval loops, not the 900 SS, and the chain guard was painted red to match the frame.

First 1984 series bodywork and chassis

Although the 1984 900 S2 frames were consistent, there were basically two types of bodywork and chassis components. There was also some overlap between types, so it's difficult to categorise these exactly by engine or frame number. Fortunately, some uniformity in component composition was evident, so it's relatively straightforward to describe the two types even if some had the later engine (with spin-on oil filter) and others the earlier type.

The colours for the first series 1984 900 S2 were black, with the same orange decals, and red, orange, and yellow stripes as before. Also unchanged were the Nippon Denso instruments, and earlier warning light panel. Some early examples had flush-mounted fairing indicators but most were on stalks. The earliest examples of this first series 1984 900 S2 still had six-spoke, gold-painted FPS aluminium wheels shod with Pirelli Phantom tyres, but some had the newer Oscam wheels with Michelin A48/M48 tubeless tyres. Most disc rotors were the earlier 900 S2 type. While the Oscam wheels offered a theoretical improvement, as they didn't require tubes for the tyres, these were an extremely heavy wheel, even heavier than the FPS.

New features for the 900 S2 this year

Some first series 1984
900 S2s had Oscam
wheels, but with the earlier
S2 discs.

included the seat covering, with a passenger strap, and silver-bodied AG Strada Marzocchi oleo-pneumatic shock absorbers. The top shock absorber bolt featured a plastic cover. Some electric start 900 S2s also included a fairing belly pan, mounted underneath the engine and located by four aluminium brackets. As it made simple maintenance tasks more complicated, the belly pan wasn't particularly practical, and another example of styling over function. The belly pan on the black 900 S2 had large orange 'DESMO' decals. The belly pan wouldn't clear the kick-start on kick-start models and wasn't fitted.

131

The final series of 900 S2 had tank badges instead of decals.
(Courtesy Two Wheels)

Second 1984 series bodywork and chassis

Production of the second 1984 series of 900 S2 coincided with the release of the new 900 Mike Hailwood Replica, and shared many components. Nearly all of this series also featured the later engine (either kick- or electric start or both) with the updated oil filter and sight glass. The red-painted frame was also unchanged.

New for this series were the colours, the bodywork painted red, with silver stripes in three shades. The paint was also higher quality this year as a new paint shop had been installed at the factory during 1983. All the other bodywork decals were silver rather than orange, with silver and black metal 'DUCATI' badges on the fuel tank. The rectangular CEV front indicators were no longer flush-mounted in the fairing, but mounted on stalks. Some bikes also came with fairing-mounted Vitaloni mirrors. The belly pan was either black or red, didn't include decals, and again not all examples were fitted with it. On those versions with the spin on oil filter the belly pan included a hole to read the oil level.

Some early examples of this second series 1984 900 S2 still had six-spoke, gold-painted FPS aluminium wheels shod with Pirelli Phantom tyres, but most had Oscam wheels with Michelin A48/M48 tubeless tyres. These wheels, tyres and brakes (drilled discs with alloy carriers) were shared with the new 900 MHR, but some 900 S2s still retained the earlier disc rotors. Others features shared with the later 1984 900 MHR included air caps on the front fork legs, a vacuum fuel tap on the right, with black neoprene rubber fuel line, and an updated warning light console between the Nippon Denso instruments. The black front mudguard on the final 900 S2 was also the 900 MHR type, solid on the front. Most of the remote-reservoir Marzocchi shock absorbers on this second series were also the black-bodied 900 MHR type. As a styling exercise the 900 S2 wasn't Ducati's most successful effort and this affected its sales and public perception. In some respects the 900 S2 was excellent, with a thoroughly sorted and reliable engine, but unfortunately the weight was up and the chassis updates poorly conceived.

1984 900 S2 distinguishing features (from engine number DM860 095742- 097200 approx. kick-start; DM860 907429-907900 approx. electric start, frame number approx. DM900SS A92400-A92800 kick-start, DM900S2 095001-097000 electric start)

Engine

New gear selector drum after engine number 095742

Saprisa three-wire alternator and regulator after number 096142

New crankcases after engine number 096314 with a spin-on oil filter and oil level sight glass

New gearbox selector drum after engine number 096314

New crankcase oil strainer after engine number 096314

Upper crankcase retaining screws 8x55mm after engine number 096314

New gear location pins for the lower timing gears after engine number 096314

Some of the final 1984 900 S2s featured a kick- and electric start

Electric start Silentium mufflers often without a kick-start indent

Chassis

Red-painted frame DM900SS for kick-start and DM900S2 for electric start

Kick-start frame numbers now began with an 'A' instead of '0'

DM900SS with DGM 13715 OM homologation DM900S2 with DGM 51148 OM

New silencer homologation plate with two numbers

Frame included a reshaped muffler bracket instead of lifting handle

Centre stand feet with loops

Red chain guard

First series with Nippon Denso instruments and earlier warning light panel

First series initially with FPS wheels and later Oscam

New seat covering with a passenger strap

Most first series with silver-bodied AG Strada Marzocchi shock absorbers

Top shock absorber bolt with a plastic cover

Some first series with a black belly pan with orange 'DESMO' decals

Some first series with flush-mounted front indicators

Second series with red bodywork with silver stripes in three shades

Second series with metal 'DUCATI' tank badges

Second series with rectangular CEV front indicators mounted on stalks

Second series with red or black belly pan was without decals

Second series mostly with Oscam wheels with drilled discs with alloy carriers

Second series with air caps on the front fork legs

Second series featured a vacuum fuel tap and black rubber fuel line

Second series included 900 MHR updated warning light console

Second series featured solid black front mudguard

Most second series with black-bodied, remote-reservoir Marzocchi shock absorbers

900 Mike Hailwood Replica

Engine

Early in 1983 work began on updating the 900 MHR. Over the previous two years the 900 MHR had been the mainstay of the Ducati bevel-drive line-up but, as with the 900 Super Sport a year earlier, its days were numbered as a kick-start only motorcycle. When the time came for an update with an electric start, Ducati chose to base the new MHR on the 900 S2 rather than the earlier SS. The new series 900 MHR was also offered as kick-start only, featuring the earlier square-case engine in the new chassis, but the majority of 1984 900 MHRs were electric start. There also wasn't a direct transition between kick-start engines with the older or new chassis, but all electric start MHRs featured the new chassis, as did the 25 kick-start 900 MHRs built in 1984. The kick-start engine was shared with the 900 S2, and all the updates covered in the previous section.

Redesigned for 1984, the 900 MHR retained strong links with earlier versions. (Courtesy Ducati Motor)

Although maintaining the same basic architecture as the existing square-case engine, the 1984 updates were the most significant since the first 860 appeared back in 1974. Developments included a dry clutch, revised electrics, a new electric start, and restyled outer engine covers. The resulting 900 was one of the finest bevel-drive engines, and even smoother and more powerful than other 900s. They were also well made as morale at the factory improved with the prospect of motorcycle manufacture continuing.

As the new engine was electric start, engine numbers continued that of the 900 S2, beginning around DM860 907000. The new crankcases also featured the same developments that appeared on the kick-start engine after DM860 096314. These included the different crankcase screws, oil level sight glass and spin-on oil filter, but there was now

an additional magnetic sump plug. The dipstick filler was removed and the hole cast over. Most of the engine internals were unchanged, including the pressed up crankshaft with 38mm crankpin, needle roller big-end bearings, one-piece forged 145mm con-rods, and 20x59mm gudgeon pin. The only difference between the new and older crankshaft was a slot machined in the right end of the crankshaft for ignition timing checking.

Although the same 9.3:1 compression ratio was maintained, the forged Cermetal NC20 86mm pistons were now matched with Gilnisil-coated cylinders without removable liners. Only two bushes were now used to locate the cylinder head with the cylinder, and there were new cylinder base gaskets. To reduce engine noise, each cylinder had 22 rubber plugs in the fins. There was no change to the design of the desmodromic cylinder head, but all valve guides were cast-iron, as were the valve seats. 25 rubber plugs were inserted between the cooling fins. The camshaft drive was unchanged, the lower bevel gear pins including the retaining circlip as on the final kick-start

engines. Apart from a new oil pump casing the oil pump was unchanged, as was the lubrication system. All electric start 900 MHRs featured a spin-on oil filter.

Although the Bosch ignition system was ostensibly unchanged, there was also a new ignition rotor on the crankshaft and the maximum advance was reduced to 28 degrees, with a static figure of five degrees. As on the 900 S2 the ignition coils were now Motoplat instead of Bosch, without the two Bosch resistors, and mounted on the front frame downtubes. The high voltage resistance was still 8800 Ohm, but the Motoplat coils were less reliable than the Bosch.

While the same helical 32/70-tooth primary drive ratio was retained, the gears were new. The flywheel was lighter, with machined flat sides, the crankshaft gear and the clutch driving gear now inboard of the steel dry clutch basket. This clutch driving gear was supported by 25x52x15mm and 25x47x12mm bearings and splined to the outer clutch drum. The hydraulically-actuated dry clutch was a significant update over earlier designs and

A dry clutch and new electric start resided underneath an attractive outer alloy cover, but the crankshaft was still a roller type on the 900 MHR.

featured a revised clutch plate layout. Similar to that of the Pantah, this now included six metal driven plates with seven friction driving plates. There was an outer metal pressure plate and six 42mm springs. Early in the 1984 model year an additional metal driven plate was added to reduce clutch slipping. The clutch actuation system through the gearbox main shaft was similar but for modifications to include the hydraulic slave cylinder. There was little change to the gearbox; the only updates were to the main shaft to incorporate the dry clutch, and an internal oil seal. The output gear was also revised to include an improved internal oil seal.

Although the basic electric start system was unchanged, there was a much smaller (and lighter) 0.7kW Nippon Denso starter motor. A lower chain drive gear accompanied this to the crankshaft drive. Although the Nippon Denso motor was troublesome on the later Mille, it had no problem starting the 864cc engine with its ball and roller bearing crankshaft. A two-piece outer clutch and primary drive cover incorporated the new electric start and dry clutch, and was accompanied by a new alternator and hydraulic slave cylinder cover on the right. The result was very attractive, and the electric start and alternator covers more compact. The alternator cover now included a removable plate with 'ELECTRONIC IGNITION' engraved on it, as well as a plastic oil filler plug. This was an unusual feature considering electronic ignition had

been featured on the bevel-drive engine for nearly 10 years, and also considering the ignition was actually on the other side of the engine.

Carburetion was by Dell'Orto PHM 40BD and BS carburettors, breathing through individual air filters as on the 900 S2. Also like the S2 the air filter boxes were painted red and breathed though normal rigid plastic intakes. The aluminium intake manifolds were now identical front and rear, although the front incorporated a special screw for a line to the vacuum fuel tap. Both carburettors had cable-operated chokes, with the plastic black lever being situated near the regulator. The exhaust system was also shared with the 900 S2 and included Silentium mufflers, although Contis were an option. For some markets a two-into-one Conti exhaust was fitted as standard, this exiting on the left. The claimed power for the new 900 was 72 horsepower at 7000rpm, with a top speed of 222km/h.

Chassis

While retaining strong visual links with the previous 900 Mike Hailwood Replica, the 1984 version was 900 S2-derived rather than Super Sport-based. Despite factory claims the new 900 MHR was heavier, longer, and taller than its predecessor. The red-painted frames for both the kick-start and electric start 1984 900 MHR were identical to the 1984 900 S2, but the frame numbers and designations differed. Although the frame differed to the previous Super Sport-type, kick-start 900 MHRs continued the DM900R series, overlapping with the earlier model and beginning around 904600. Electric start models had a new frame designation, DM 900R1, the numbers beginning at 905002 (905001 was a factory test example). The electric start frame also featured a different frame homologation number, DGM 51147 OM. The kick-start version retained the earlier DGM 50235 OM homologation number but some electric start 900 MHRs had the kick-start frame homologation number, along with the electric start designation and sequence. The frame included a Neiman steering head lock and lifting handle incorporated in the shape of the muffler bracket. There was a longer centre stand with two springs. The black silencer homologation number on the right, underneath the side cover, was new, and different from the 900 S2, but also with two numbers (E3 41R 0040039 for Silentium and E3 13R 0440038 for Contis).

A taller and narrower fibreglass two-piece fairing set the 1984 900 MHR apart from earlier versions. The improved design allowed for easier removal of the lower section, and was retained by eight 6x18mm and eight 6x16mm chrome-plated screws. A hole was provided on the right to check the oil level and, because the fairing was split horizontally, the positioning of the decals differed. Although the style (and decals) of the 24-litre steel fuel tank and seat arrangement followed that of the 1983 series, the tank included a lockable fuel cap and new fuel taps. This was a combination of a vacuum tap on the right and a manual tap (with reserve) on the left, and there were also black rubber fuel lines. The ABS seat unit sometimes featured a 'DESMO' decal on the rear, and there were two different seat patterns. One was pleated and the other had stamped squares, both types also featuring a passenger grab strap. There were also new slotted ABS side covers with '900' decals. The black mudguards were similar in shape to those of the 600 SL Pantah, with the front of ABS and the rear of steel with a black plastic front section. Although the tank decals were often crooked, the paint was higher quality this year and included a clear coating over the decals. Some 1984 900 MHRs came with Vitaloni fairing-mounted rear-view mirrors.

The Marzocchi suspension was shared with the final series 900 S2, the front fork with 38x590mm fork tubes, 221mm hydraulic rods, black-painted fork legs, and rear-mounted brake calipers. During 1984 the fork finish changed to matte black with new top fork leg oil seals to further improve the fork action. These no longer included the outer fork cups but retained the usual yellow Marzocchi decal on the left. At the same time the forks gained air caps with a Schrader valve on the top of each leg. Also shared with the 900 S2 were twin, black-bodied, five-way adjustable AG Strada oleo-pneumatic Marzocchi shock absorbers providing a 75mm stroke. All the wheels on this series of 900 MHR were gold-painted aluminium Oscam, with tubeless Michelin A48 and M48 tyres. As on the 900 S2 the cush drive rubber was now without the hard round inserts, and the 33-tooth rear sprocket retained with five 8x40mm Allen bolts with Nyloc nuts, without lock plates. The chain guard was black and not red as on the 900 S2.

The 1984 900 MHR fairing was taller and narrower than before. (Courtesy Ducati Victor)

Also shared with the 900 S2 was the Brembo braking system, with black 08 brake calipers with a single bleed nipple and plastic pad covers. The front brake calipers were mounted behind the fork legs and the discs were as on the 1983 900 MHR. These were six-bolt, 280mm, drilled cast-iron with aluminium carriers with large relieved holes. The front master cylinder differed between kick- and electric start versions, the electric start model sharing its master cylinder with the 600 SL Pantah and featuring a black dogleg lever. The rear brake was also the same as the 900 S2, the master cylinder with a remote reservoir located beneath the right-hand side cover.

There were different handlebars and levers for the kick- and electric start versions. The kick-start version featured chrome-plated, forward-set, clip-on handlebars similar to those on the 900 SSD

Oscam wheels with tubeless tyres were fitted to the 1984 900 MHR. (Courtesy Ducati Motor)

As the clutch was still cable-operated, the black clutch lever, bracket, and adjustment mechanism was as on the 1983 900 MHR. The black brake lever was also from the earlier model, as were the Verlicchi handgrips.

New black Verlicchi clip-on handlebars set the electric start 900 MHR apart. These were also forward-set, but provided adjustment in three planes. The clutch master cylinder (with black dog-leg lever) was on the left handlebar, and the plastic twin-cable Verlicchi throttle was the 900 S2 type, incorporating the starter button and engine stop switch. Most of the frame fittings were from the 900 S2, including the aluminium foot levers and the folding footpegs with rubbers. The gearshift and brake pedals used the earlier rubbers, these changing to a ribbed type during 1984. The gearshift linkage still used a balljoint with a clevis pin, and the passenger footpegs were the newer 900 S2 type.

The electrical system was similar to the 900 S2, but the electric start version featured some updates. This included a 170mm Carello H4 60W headlamp and a revised instrument panel with eight LED warning lamps under an opaque cover. Designed for the impending Mille, the fuel and oil pressure indicators weren't connected on the 900. Kick-start versions retained the earlier warning light arrangement between the Nippon Denso speedometer and tachometer. Both kick- and electric start models shared the larger CEV taillight and stalk-mounted indicators with the 900 S2.

Although the 1984 900 MHR was considered an interim model, many more electric start versions (1457) were produced than the later Mille. By 1984 the Mike Hailwood Replica was really an anachronism as 18in wheels and twin shock absorber rear suspension was unfashionable. This year was a transitional one for Ducati as it moved towards Cagiva ownership and the 900 MHR was a confused product. While the engine demonstrated the finest aspects of a decade of evolution, the chassis was seemingly designed to appease style and practicality. The result was a motorcycle functionally inferior to its predecessor, but one that would see the bevel-drive engine through until its demise.

As on the 900 S2 the rear master cylinder had a hidden reservoir. (Courtesy Ducati Motor)

Although retaining Nippon Denso instruments, the dash layout of the 1984 900 MHR featured a new warning light panel. (Courtesy Ducati Motor)

It may have been obsolete by 1984 but the 900 MHR was still a handsome machine.

1984 900 MHR distinguishing features (from engine number DM860 096314-097200 approx. kick-start; DM860 907000-909500 approx. electric start, frame number approx. DM900R 904600-904750 kick-start, DM900R1 905002-906500 electric start)

Engine

Electric start crankcases with oil level sight glass, spin-on oil filter, and magnetic sump plug
Slot machined in the right end of the crankshaft for ignition timing checking
Gilnisil-coated cylinders without removable liners
Only two bushes used to locate the cylinder head with the cylinder
Rubber plugs in cylinder and cylinder head cooling fins
New oil pump casing
New ignition rotor and maximum advance was reduced to 28 degrees
Motoplat ignition coils
Lighter flywheel, with machined flat sides
Hydraulically-actuated dry clutch
Smaller 0.7kW Nippon Denso starter motor
A two-piece outer clutch and primary drive
New electric start and dry clutch cover
New alternator and hydraulic slave cylinder cover on the right

Chassis

Red-painted frame shared with the 1984 900 S2
Kick-start frame the DM900R series with DGM 50235 OM homologation number
Electric start frame with DM 900R1 and DGM 51147 OM homologation number
New silencer homologation numbers E3 41R 0040039 and E3

13R 0440038
Taller and narrower fibreglass two-piece fairing
New fuel taps, a vacuum tap on the right, with black rubber fuel lines
Two types of seat pattern
Slotted ABS side covers with '900' decals
Black mudguards
During 1984 matte black fork legs with new seals
During 1984 forks fitted with a Schrader valve on the top of each leg
Black-bodied AG Strada oleo-pneumatic Marzocchi shock absorbers
Gold-painted aluminium Oscam wheels with tubeless Michelin A48 and M48 tyres
Black chain guard
Front brake calipers mounted behind the fork legs
Six-bolt 280mm drilled discs with aluminium carriers with large relieved holes
Rear brake master cylinder with a remote reservoir
Electric start models with dogleg handlebar levers
Electric start models with adjustable Verlicchi clip-on handlebars
Electric start models with plastic twin-cable Verlicchi throttle
170mm Carello H4 60W headlamp
Revised instrument panel with eight LED warning lamps under an opaque cover
Larger CEV taillight and stalk-mounted indicators

CHAPTER TWELVE

1985-1986

The Mille MHR was very similar looking to the previous 900 MHR.

Although it was initially planned for Ducati to cease motorcycle production during 1985, the agreement with Cagiva was slower in its implementation than had been envisaged. By early 1985 Ducati's management was still resisting pressure from Cagiva to cease motorcycle manufacture in preference for engines only. As a result, motorcycle production continued, albeit on a much reduced scale. When the purchase of Ducati was finalised during 1985 Cagiva eventually relented, retaining the Bologna plant for complete motorcycle manufacture, and also deciding to keep the Ducati name. The future of the bevel-drive bikes was less certain, but soon after buying Ducati Cagiva engaged Massimo Tamburini to design a chrome-molybdenum square-section steel frame for the Mille engine. This also featured a 'full-floater'-style, rising rate, single Öhlins shock absorber aluminium swingarm, with rear axle eccentrics for chain adjustment. Other components included a Marzocchi M1R 41.7mm front fork with rebound damping in one leg and compression damping in the other, and 16in wheels. The exhausts were upswept and hidden underneath the bodywork. Weighing 205kg, the specification of the Tamburini Mille was impressive and promised excellent performance with a claimed top speed of around 230km/h. Unfortunately, this exciting bike was due to appear at the 1985 Milan Show but didn't get past the prototype stage. The chassis formed the basis up the new 750 Paso that appeared at Milan instead. Cagiva also built a prototype 900 'Americano' Harley-Davidson-style chopper during 1985. This was originally slated for production in late 1986 but didn't eventuate. By early 1986 Cagiva had decided the bevel-twin uneconomic to produce and would have difficulty meeting future noise and emission requirements.

1000 'Mille' Mike Hailwood Replica

Work on the Mille bevel-twin began as soon as the V-four project was scrapped, sometime prior to the Cagiva agreement. Ing. Fabio Taglioni and his new assistant Ing. Massimo Bordi began the development of the Mille engine during 1983, seemingly oblivious to the political machinations surrounding them. Considering the cost of producing the bevel-drive engine it was surprising that Fabio Taglioni persuaded the managing director, Cosimo Calcagnile, to allow further improvement of his venerable design. When asked about this Taglioni replied, "Unlike some other directors Calcagnile had been with Ducati many years and he appreciated the historical importance of this engine." By early 1984 the prototype engine was running and soon installed in an S2 chassis (with 16in wheels) for testing. A second prototype was a Mike Hailwood Replica, in red and yellow, with black Oscam wheels and a two-into-one Cont exhaust system.

Engine

The Mille engine was conceived in two stages, the first with redesigned outer engine covers and a dry clutch, and the second with larger displacement and a plain bearing crankshaft. The first stage updates featured on the 1984 900 MHR, with the second stage following later in 1984 with the Mille. The Mille also gained a new set of engine numbers, starting at ZDM1000 100001, finishing around ZDM1000 101350. ZDM was the prefix required for international VIN identification. Engines were also shared with the Mille S2, and some of the final versions had an 'L' stamped next to the number. Except for the lubrication system the aluminium crankcases were basically as for the 1984 900 MHR. The lubrication system now included a larger spin-on oil filter, with an oil pressure switch and a bypass valve.

Although visually similar to the 1984 900 MHR motor, the Mille engine included a number of significant updates. The 900 engine was bored and stroked, the 88x78mm dimensions providing a 109cc increase, to 973cc. Racing engines had been using 90mm pistons for several years, but this required considerable modification to the crankcases and cylinder heads, while 88mm could be accommodated quite comfortably. The Mille barrel flange was 6mm wide and the cylinder head studs nicely waisted to provide clearance for the slightly larger cylinders. As on the 1984 900 MHR

One of the new engine features were the special cylinder studs.

the Mille's 88mm cylinders were Gilnisil-treated aluminium, without the earlier cast-iron sleeves, and there were no large retaining dowels between the cylinder and cylinder head.

As the bore was only increased by 2mm, the cylinder head castings were unchanged, retaining the older 80 degree included valve angle and the same 100mm head recess diameter. Taglioni wanted to include 60 degree cylinder heads like the Pantah, but this was vetoed by Calcagnile as they were deemed too expensive. With endurance racing and TT1 heading towards a 750cc limit in 1984 Ducati saw no future in the Mille as a racing engine anyway. The valve sizes were increased slightly, with the intake valve now 42mm and the exhaust valve 38mm. The valve seats were larger to accommodate the valves, but all the other cylinder head specifications were unchanged, including camshafts. Although early Mille engines included the 900 cylinder head camshaft bearing housings, later examples featured a new housing. These were fitted sometime around engine number 100700.

The most important update on the Mille engine was the new crankshaft. A relic of its conceptual days, the pressed together roller bearing crankshaft had long been the Achilles Heel of the bevel-drive engine. Back in 1970 when Fabio Taglioni first conceived the V-twin motor he was reluctant to build a high performance engine with a plain-bearing, one-piece crankshaft. Many British parallel twins were suffering plain-bearing crankshaft problems, and the new BMW 5-series was yet to prove itself. Although the Moto Guzzi V7 had proved reliable Taglioni didn't feel this was a true high performance design. Taglioni was a traditionalist and the 750 twin incorporated many 1950s racing design features. This included the bevel-drive layout, wide 80 degree included valve angle, and ball and roller bearing crankshaft.

While the V-twin crankshaft assembly was creditably reliable in the low compression 750 GT, it became a cause for concern under racing conditions and with the larger capacity 860 GT and 900 Super Sport. Even the redesigned crankpin and bearings that were introduced with the 900 SD in 1977 failed to increase the service life dramatically. Ironically it was the disastrous parallel twin of 1975 that changed Taglioni's thinking on plain bearing crankshafts. Taglioni was strongly opposed to the parallel twin, having nothing to do with it, and Ing. Tumidei was left to his own devices. When designing the twin Tumidei broke with Ducati tradition, and included a plain-bearing crankshaft. While the engine had plenty of shortcomings, the crank assembly wasn't one of them and it soon emerged as one of the most reliable components in the engine. Taglioni initially produced his new Pantah engine with a roller bearing crankshaft, but when he saw the reliability of the crankshaft in the parallel twin decided to follow that path. In 1977 the prototype Pantah gained a one-piece crankshaft with plain big-end bearings while retaining the high speed angular contact ball main bearings. This was also extremely reliable and, after the Pantah went into production in 1979, it was soon apparent that the big-end problems of previous Ducati V-twins were a thing of the past.

With this in mind Taglioni decided to install a Pantah-style crankshaft in the Mille. The crankpin journal grew from 38mm to 45mm, with a corresponding increase in rigidity, and with this crankshaft it was also relatively easy to increase the stroke by 3.6mm (to 78mm). Retaining the angular thrust ball main bearings of the previous engine, the crankshaft was shimmed for zero end float on both sides rather than only on the drive side as before. The bearings also required preload. The con-rods were two-piece, and the con-rod bearings made of Clevite CL112, the highest grade available in Italy at the time. To retain the same external engine dimensions the con-rod length was unchanged at 145mm. This provided a stroke/bore ratio of only 1.81 compared to 1.95 but, as this was a street engine with a 7500rpm

limit, Taglioni didn't feel this was a problem. The increase in angular con-rod movement due to the extreme con-rod length to stroke ratio was also not as critical with plain bearings. To provide con-rod clearance the forged, three-ring, 88mm, 9.3:1 pistons had 2mm shorter skirts, with the gudgeon pins located nearer the crown.

Although the square-case camshaft gear drive system was retained, the oil pump was considerably uprated. The 38-tooth oil pump drive gear was now driven directly from the 28-tooth crankshaft gear as the larger oil pump body didn't allow room for the additional drive gear. There was also an updated gear support plate. The oil pump design was much as before, but used two, wider (20mm) 11-tooth gears to provide an oil flow of 18.3-litres per minute. Oil pressure was increased to around 80psi, up from around 20-25psi for the previous roller bearing engine. After engine number 100388 there was a new oil pump body. The oil pump lines were sealed with two O-rings, but while the oil pressure was increased for the plain big-end bearings the lubrication system was unchanged. This still wasn't a full-flow filtration system like that of the Pantah, with all the oil filtered before going to the crankshaft and cylinder heads. After engine number 100129 there was an oil flow reducing plug fitted to the front cylinder. While the Bosch ignition and Motoplat coils were unchanged, there was a revised ignition pickup plate and all-metal engine side cover plugs for the ignition and alternator wires.

To reduce the torque on the gearbox the primary drive ratio was raised, speeding the clutch basket. The helical primary gears were now 39- and 69-tooth, providing a ratio of 1.769:1. As all the dry clutch updates featured on the 1984 900 MHR there were only small changes to the clutch for the Mille. These included a new outside pressure plate and shorter (40mm) clutch springs. The pressure plate no longer had an external threaded adjustment screw.

Accompanying the new primary drive was a new gearbox. Although the fourth and fifth gear ratios were unchanged, direct drive fourth gear was strengthened. The three lower ratios were widened, presumably to help the dry clutch in first gear. The design of the three-dog gearbox was as before, but there was a new main shaft and secondary shaft, as well as main shaft third and fifth gears. First gear was now 17/37, second 22/31, and third 27/27, all with the 24/30 drive to the main shaft. With first gear providing a 1.270:1 reduction and second a 1.761:1 reduction there was a large gap between first and second gears. The gap from second to the 1.250:1 third gear was also quite large and these wide gearbox ratios compromised the Mille as a sporting motorcycle. As the gearbox rotated faster the gear selector forks featured hard-chromed ends to minimise wear. Accompanying this was a redesigned selector detent mechanism with a ball and stronger spring, and a new secondary shaft bearing in the left crankcase. A gutter in the left crankcase casting, just in front of the layshaft bearing, now collected oil splashed from the primary drive. This was routed to the gearbox layshaft where it provided additional lubrication for the selector forks.

Taglioni and Bordi obviously expected problems with the 900 MHR's electric start mechanism as, while retaining the small Nippon Denso starter motor, they revised the drive gears to provide an improved starting ratio. This still wasn't enough to overcome the additional friction of the

plain bearings and larger cylinders, and the Mille often remained a reluctant starter. The Mille also included a cap over the electric start motor bearing, and a slightly different primary drive cover.

The Dell'Orto PHM 40B carburettors featured identical jetting to those on the 1984 900 MHR along with an identical air cleaner system. The air filter boxes were also painted red on earlier examples, later changing to black. Because the jetting was the same as for the 900, some Milles exhibited a tendency to hunt on partial throttle. Apart from new clamps, the exhaust system with Silentium mufflers was also identical to that of the final 900. Contis were no longer listed as an official option, although they were an easy installation. The Mille engine provided only a modest increase in power over the 900, to a claimed 76 horsepower at 6700rpm, but a massive increase in torque. Torque increased from the 7.9 kilogram meters at

The tall and narrow profile presented by the Mille MHR was beginning to date by 1985. (Courtesy Two Wheels)

143

6000rpm of the 900 to 8.6 kilogram meters at only 5500rpm for the Mille. The top speed of 222km/h was unchanged.

Chassis

Only small details separated the chassis and cycle parts from those of the 1984 900 MHR. The red-painted frame and swingarm were identical to those on the 1984 900 MHR (with the same part number), but carried a new frame number sequence and homologation number. As with other models after the Cagiva buy-out there was a ZDM prefix, with numbers beginning at ZDM1000R 100001. The new frame homologation number was DGM 51429 OM and there were also new silencer homologation numbers, E3 41R 0040605 and E3 13R 0440604.

All the bodywork was similar to the 1984 900 MHR. Specific updates included 'Mille' decals

The earliest Mille MHRs had black-painted fork legs and the 900 camshaft bearing housings.

on the fairing (although some early examples came with '1000' decals), and 'DESMO' decals on the side covers. Although the fuel tank was unchanged, most Mille MHRs came with a black lockable fuel filler cap. The 'DUCATI' tank decals were mostly crooked. The fairing included a new plexiglass screen, and the ABS rear seat section and thicker rear solo seat pad were new. A white 'DUCATI' decal was on the rear of the seat unit instead of the earlier 'DESMO'. The fairing and side cover screws were black, and the ABS front mudguard was red. This was similar in design to that of the 1984 900 MHR but with a solid front section.

While retaining the 221mm hydraulic brake rod, to increase ground clearance, the 38mm Marzocchi fork had longer fork tubes. On early examples the fork legs and triple clamps were painted black, but most Mille MHRs had red-painted fork legs and triple clamps. The fork sealing now featured a single oil seal along

with internal dust seals and each fork leg had an individual Schrader air valve. There was no change to the black Marzocchi AG Strada shock absorbers.

Although there had been experimentation with 16in wheels on a prototype these didn't make the production version. The 1984 900 MHR's 18in Oscam wheels were retained, identical but for a new cush drive flange. Some of the very last 1986 Mille MHRs had a new type of 18in Oscam wheel, with a revised three-spoke pattern. The tyres were as for 1984, tubeless Michelin A/M48, the rear now a larger section 130/80V18. There was no change to the Brembo braking system, and to allow for the higher primary drive gearing the final drive was lowered considerably, with a 106-link chain and 15- and 41-tooth sprockets. The black chain guard was angled higher to provide clearance for the larger rear sprocket.

There was a new wiring loom for the Mille MHR but this was similar in design to the 1984 900 MHR. Included next to the battery was an additional decal warning not to run the engine with the battery disconnected. Either a 12V 24Ah or 12V 19Ah battery was fitted. Other equipment was as with the final 900 MHR, although the oil pressure warning light on the dashboard was connected.

During 1985 an evolutionary Mille MHR was tested, with a 16in front Oscam wheel from a 750 F1, and a Marzocchi M1R front fork. The fairing included a rectangular headlight with two cooling scoops, and the colours were red and yellow. This prototype didn't make it past the testing stage and the Mille Mike Hailwood Replica ended in early 1986, with a final 250 built. Even by this stage it was undecided whether to cease production as a number of Mille MHRs were seen at the factory in January 1986 with new Cagiva elephant decals. There was a considerable number of Mille MHRs stockpiled at this time, all retaining the earlier Giugiaro-style decals. 25 late examples were modified by Gerold Vogel in Weinfelden, Switzerland and offered for sale during 1988. They incorporated small detail touches that included a half fairing, Fabio Taglioni-signed engine covers in red, white-faced Nippon Denso instruments, and red-painted, three-spoke Oscam wheels.

1000 'Mille' S2

Produced alongside the Mille Mike Hailwood Replica was the similar Mille S2. As the 900 S2 was never a runaway success this offering was unusual, but someone high up at Ducati obviously liked the S2. An S2 with 16in wheels was used as a test bed for the Mille engine and, apart from the bodywork, the S2 was identical to the MHR. The engines of the Mille S2 and MHR were shared, with the same

All Mille MHRs had an air valve on each fork leg. The plastic Verlicchi throttle featured on all electric start bevel-twins from the 900 S2.

This Mille MHR with Cagiva lettering was photographed at the factory in January 1986.

The prototype Mille MHR with a 16-inch wheel, unveiled in 1995 by long-time Ducati mechanic Giuliano Pedretti.

1985-86 1000 MHR distinguishing features (from engine number ZDM1000 100001-101350 approx., frame number ZDM1000R 100001-101150 approx.)

Engine

Engine numbers from ZDM1000 100001
Some final engines with an 'L' stamped next to the number
Larger oil filter, oil pressure switch, and bypass valve
88x78mm providing 973cc
Waisted cylinder head studs
Gilnisil-treated aluminium cylinders
No large retaining dowels between the cylinder and cylinder head
42mm intake and 38mm exhaust valves
Later engines with new camshaft bearing housings (after 100700 approx.)
One-piece crankshaft with 45mm crankpin journal
Two-piece 145mm con-rods
Pistons with 2mm shorter skirts and higher gudgeon pin location
Uprated oil pump with the oil pump drive gear driven directly from crankshaft
Updated gear support plate
Oil pump with two 20mm 11 tooth gears
New oil pump body after engine number 100388
Oil flow reducing plug after engine number 100129
All-metal engine side cover ignition and alternator plugs
Higher primary gear ratio with 39- and 69-tooth gears
New clutch outside pressure plate and shorter clutch springs
Strengthened fourth gear
Lower first three gear ratios
Hard-chromed gear selector fork ends
Redesigned selector detent mechanism

New layshaft bearing in the left crankcase
Gutter in the left crankcase casting to lubricate the selector forks
New electric start drive gears to provide an improved starting ratio
Cap over the electric start motor bearing
Different primary drive cover
Red air filter boxes later changing to black

Chassis

Red-painted frame identical to the 1984 900 MHR
Frame numbers beginning at ZDM1000R 100001
New frame homologation number DGM 51429 OM
New silencer homologation numbers E3 41R 0040605 and E3 13R 0440604
'Mille' or '1000' fairing decals and 'DESMO' side cover decals
Most with black lockable fuel filler cap
'DUCATI' decal on the rear of the seat unit
Black fairing and side cover screws
Red front mudguard with solid front section
Longer fork tubes
Early fork legs and triple clamps painted black, later painted red
New rear wheel cush drive flange
Some of the last examples with a three-spoke Oscam wheels
Larger section 130/80V18 rear tyre
Black chain guard was angled higher
Oil pressure warning light on the dashboard connected

ZDM 1000 prefix and series, and S2 engines after around 100700 included the later camshaft bearing supports. The Mille S2 didn't prove especially popular and only 171 were produced, 71 in 1984 and 100 in 1985. Production began slightly after the Mille MHR, engine numbers beginning around 100250. The Mille S2 also finished before the Mille MHR, around engine number 100950 (although frame numbers were often much lower).

Although the red-painted frame was identical to that of the Mille MHR, it initially carried a new frame number designation, ZDM1000S2. Numbers began at 100001, ending around 100125. After around 100125 the ZDM1000S2 frame designation was discarded and subsequent Mille S2s used the ZDM1000R frame and number of the Mille MHR. These numbers began around 100400, through until approximately 100650. There was some overlap between the 1000S2 and 1000R frame, with some very late Mille S2s receiving a 1000S2 frame and some early examples (built 1984) with

a 1000R frame. The frame homologation number (DGM 51429 OM) was the same for both types, as were the silencer homologation numbers. Shorter steering head stops provided the Mille S2 frame more steering lock.

The black Mille S2 bodywork was patterned on that of the first series 1984 900 S2. While the steel fuel tank was the same, with orange decals, the fuel taps were the vacuum and manual type of the second 1984 series. Mille S2s came with a black belly pan under the engine (with orange 'DESMO' decals), black-plated screws retaining the bodywork, and a black ABS front mudguard with a solid front section. The fairing was similar to the previous 900 S2 but no longer required a cut-out for the electric start motor, as this smaller unit required less clearance.

All Mille S2s came with red-painted fork legs and triple clamps. The front fork had a yellow Marzocchi decal at the base of the left leg and the fork legs had individual air caps. As on the Mille

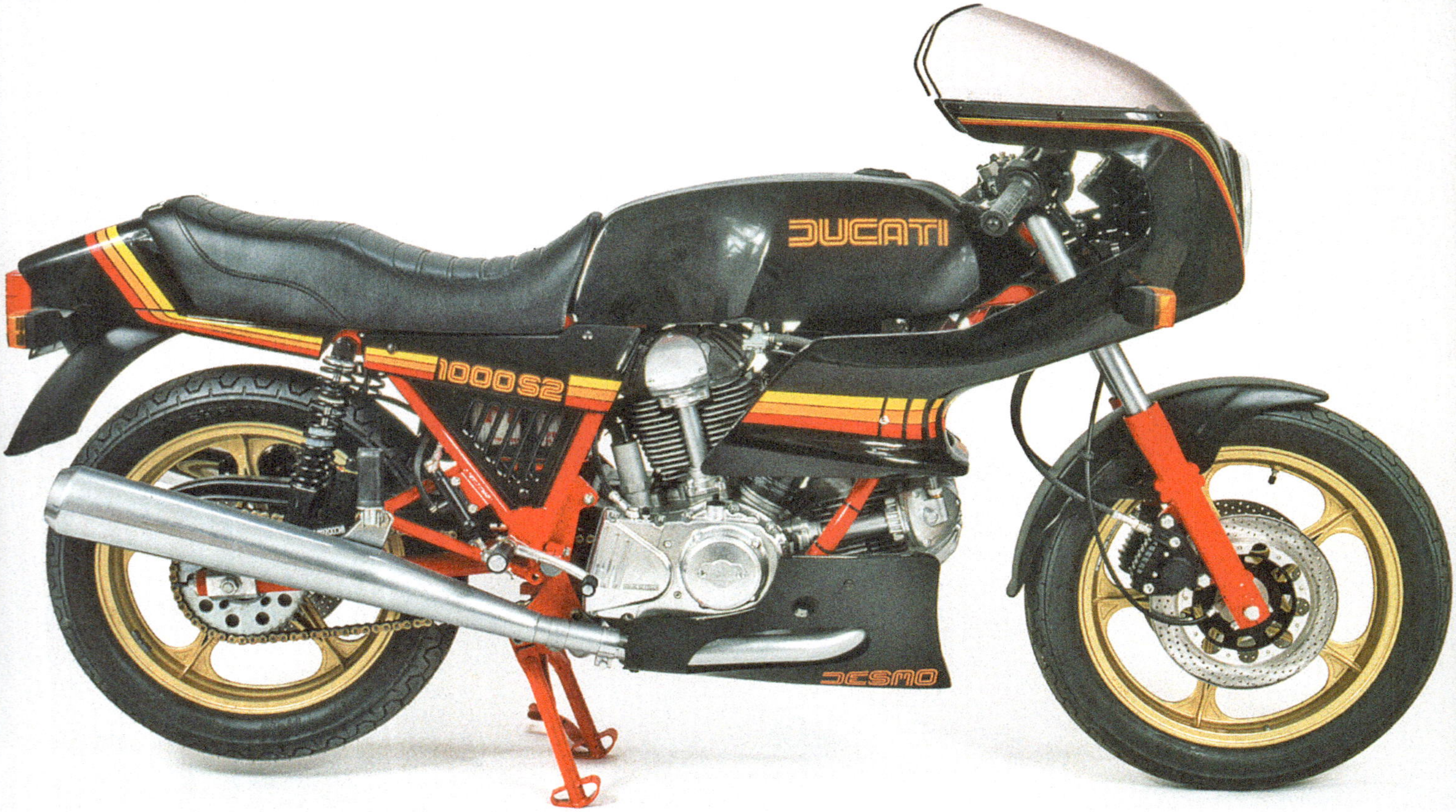

The Mille S2 continued the style of the 900 S2, but the colours and decals were as for the first 1984 900 S2 series. (Courtesy Ducati Motor)

Mille engine after around 100700 featured updated camshaft bearing supports.

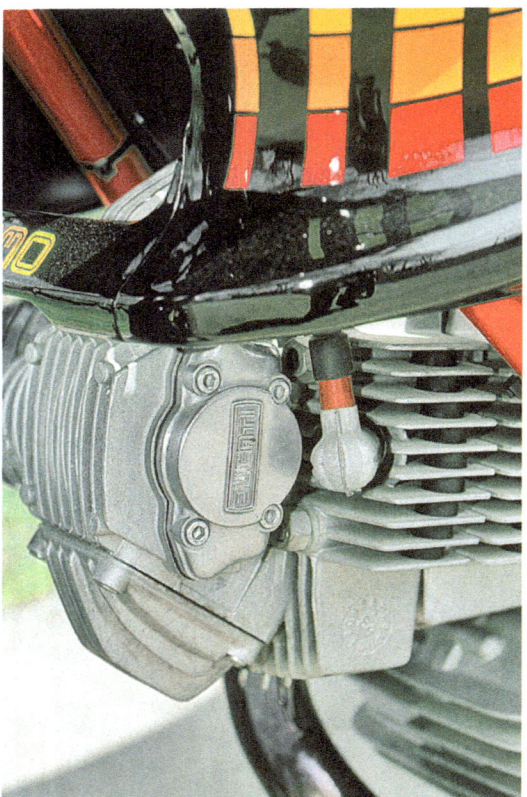

MHR the fork tubes were longer than on the 900. The Oscam wheels, Brembo brakes, Michelin tyres (130/80V18 on the rear), and black chain guard were as for the Mille MHR. Instead of the 900 S2's Bosch headlight the Mille S2 shared the Carello headlamp of the Mille MHR, along with the adjustable Verlicchi handlebars, black dog-leg levers and instrument panel. The front rectangular CEV indicators were on stalks, and some Mille S2s were fitted with a larger 24Ah battery.

While the factory no longer considered the bevel-drive engine suitable for Endurance or TT1 racing, there was still life left in it for the Battle of the Twins. In the US, Reno Leoni switched from a Cagiva Pantah in 1985 to a Mille for 1986 and 1987. Leoni bored the engine to 1017cc to produce more than 100 horsepower at the rear wheel. Running 16in wheels, Adamo led the 1987 Daytona BOTT race before retiring. But the reality was the bevel-drive engine was always going to be limited in absolute power output and, by 1987, a totally new engine generation was about to be unleashed, the 851 Desmoquattro that would also relegate the Pantah obsolete. After all the improvements implemented with the Mille engine it was unfortunate that its release coincided with the Cagiva buy-out. While Cagiva undoubtedly saved Ducati, the Castiglionis were pragmatic

The Mille S2 fairing didn't require a cutout to allow clearance for the electric start motor.

businessmen and the expensive bevel-drive engine was the first casualty. With the death of the Mille one of the most significant engine series in the history of Ducati ignominiously ended.

Although there have been great Ducati engines since, few have been as charismatic as the bevel-drive twin.

This Mille S2 has an optional Conti two-into-one exhaust system, and hence no belly pan.

1985 1000 S2 distinguishing features (from engine number ZDM1000 100250-100950 approx., frame number ZDM1000S2 100001-10125 approx. ZDM1000R 100400-100650 approx.)

Red-painted frame identical to the 1984 900 MHR
Frame numbers beginning at ZDM1000R 100001
New frame homologation number DGM 51429 OM
New silencer homologation numbers E3 41R 0040605 and
  E3 13R 0440604
'Mille' or '1000' fairing decals and 'DESMO' side cover decals
Most with black lockable fuel filler cap
'DUCATI' decal on the rear of the seat unit
Black fairing and side cover screws

Red front mudguard with solid front section
Longer fork tubes
Early fork legs and triple clamps painted black, later
  painted red
New rear wheel cush drive flange
Some of the last examples with three-spoke Oscam wheels
Larger section 130/80V18 rear tyre
Black chain guard was angled higher
Oil pressure warning light on the dashboard connected

APPENDIX

The specifications listed are official factory figures. As sources, workshop manuals have been used in preference to owners' manuals

Specifications Ducati 860 GT/GTE 1975

Motor denomination	DM860
Frame homologation	DM860S
Homologation certificate	DGM 13715 OM
Engine type	Two-cylinder, four-stroke, 90 degree 'L' twin
Bore	86mm
Stroke	74.4mm
Capacity	863.9cc
Compression ratio	9:1 (workshop manual; 9.5:1 in owners' manual)
Valve distribution	Two valves inclined at 80 degrees, driven by single overhead camshafts
Valve timing (inlet)	Inlet opens 48 degrees BTDC, closes 83 degrees ABDC (clearance0.08mm)
Valve timing (exhaust)	Exhaust opens 83 degrees BBDC, closes 48 degrees ATDC (clearance 0.12mm)
Carburettors	2 Dell'Orto PHF32AD/AS, 122 main jet, 60 pilot jet, 70/2 slide, K6 needle 2nd notch, 265AB needle jet
Lubrication	Wet sump, gear drive
Ignition	Electronic, automatic advance 28 degrees at 2000rpm, total advance 35-38 degrees
Spark plugs	Champion L88A
Electrical system	12V, 150W alternator until 851683, 200W from 851684, electronic current regulator
Battery	Yuasa 12N-12A-4A, Yuasa B68-12V-36Ah (GTE)
Primary drive	Helical gear (32/70) 1:2.187
Clutch	Wet multiplate
Transmission	Five-speed constant mesh
First	1:2.237 (19/34 x 24/30)
Second	1:1.562 (24/30 x 24/30)
Third	1:1.204 (27/26 x 24/30)
Fourth	1:1.000 direct drive
Fifth	1:0.887 (31/22 x 24/30)
Secondary drive	1:2.500 (16/40) $\frac{5}{8}$x$\frac{3}{8}$in Renold chain 108 links
Frame	Tubular steel, open double cradle with crankcases acting as frame member
Front suspension	Ceriani 38mm telescopic fork
Rear suspension	Twin Marzocchi 320mm shock absorbers, three-way adjustable for spring preload
Front wheel	Radaelli WM3x18 40 spoke steel
Front tyre	3.50H18 Pirelli MT18, Metzeler C66
Front tyre pressure	2.2-2.3kg/cm² (31.3-32.7lb/sq.in)
Rear wheel	Radaelli WM3x18 40-spoke steel
Rear tyre	120/90 H18 Pirelli MT18, 4.00x18 Metzeler C66
Rear tyre pressure	2.5-2.7kg/cm² (35.6-38.4lb/sq.in)
Front brake	Brembo P2F08N twin piston caliper, Brembo 15.8mm master cylinder, 280mm disc (twin disc option)
Rear brake	200mm single leading-shoe

Front fork capacity	210cc (180-185cc owners' manual) AGIP OSO 25 in each leg	First	1:2.237 (13/34 x 24/30)
Oil sump capacity	5-litres Agip F 1 Racing S 50	Second	1:1.562 (24/30 x 24/30)
Fuel tank capacity	18-litres, reserve 2-litres (17-litres owners' manual)	Third	1:1.204 (27/26 x 24/30)
		Fourth	1:1.000 direct drive
Wheelbase	1520mm	Fifth	1:0.887 (31/22 x 24/30)
Length	2200mm	Secondary drive	750 SS 1:2.500 (16/40) ⅝x⅜in
Max. height	1170mm		Renold BS chain
Max. width	900mm		900 SS 1:2.312 (16/37); 1:2.250
Ground clearance	180mm		(16/36)
Seat height	800mm	Front Suspension	Marzocchi 38 mm telescopic fork
Dry weight	206kg, 217kg (GTE)		(280cc ATF Dexron per leg)
		Rear suspension	Twin Marzocchi 320mm shock
			absorbers, five-way adjustable for
			spring preload

Colours 860 GT/GTE

Bodywork	Stripe
Orange	Black
Red	White
Black	White
Blue	White
Yellow	Black
Green	White

		Front wheel	Borrani WM3x18 40-spoke steel
		Front tyre	Metzeler 3.50V18 Block C7 Racing
		Front tyre pressure	2.4-2.5kg/cm² (34.85 lb/sq.in)
		Rear wheel	Borrani WM3x18 40-spoke steel
		Rear tyre	Metzeler 3.50V18 Block C7 Racing
		Rear tyre pressure	2.6-2.7kg/cm² (37.69 lb/sq.in)
		Front brake	Twin Brembo P2F08N twin piston caliper, Brembo 15.8mm master cylinder 280mm discs

Specifications Ducati 750/900 Super Sport 1975

Motor denomination	DM750.1, (DM860.1)	Rear brake	Brembo P2F08N twin-piston caliper, 229mm disc
Frame homologation	DM750SS	Front fork capacity	280cc AGIP ATF Dexron in each leg
Homologation certificate	DGM 11871 OM	Oil sump capacity	4.5kg Agip F 1 Racing S 50
Bore	80mm (86mm; 900)	Fuel tank capacity	20-litres (2.5-litre reserve)
Stroke	74.4mm	Wheelbase	1500mm
Capacity	748cc (863.9cc; 900)	Length	2220mm
Max engine rpm	8800 (750); 7900 (900)	Max. height	1230mm
Compression ratio	9:65:1 (9.5:1; 900)	Max. width	675mm
Valve distribution	Two desmodromic valves inclined at 80 degrees, driven by single overhead camshafts	Ground clearance	180mm
		Seat height	770mm
Valve timing (Inlet)	Inlet opens 63 degrees BTDC, closes 83 degrees ABDC (opening clearance 0.13mm, closing 0.00mm)	Dry weight	188kg (750 SS), 187kg (900 SS)

Specifications Ducati 860/900 GTS 1976-79 (differing from 860 GTE)

Valve timing (Exhaust)	Exhaust opens 80 degrees BBDC, closes 58 degrees ATDC (opening clearance 0.15mm, closing 0.00mm)	Valve timing	(Inlet) From number 853788 Inlet opens 51 degrees BTDC, closes 75 degrees ABDC (clearance 0.08mm)
Carburettors	2 Dell'Orto PHM40AD/AS, 152 main jet, 60 pilot jet, 60/1 slide, K4 needle 2nd notch, 265AB needle jet	Valve timing	(Exhaust) from number 853788 Exhaust opens 74 degrees BBDC, closes 46 degrees ATDC (clearance 0.12mm)
Ignition	Electronic, automatic advance 28 degrees at 2000rpm, total advance 35-38 degrees	Electrical system	12V, 200W electronic current regulator
Spark plugs	Champion L81 (0.8mm gap)	Battery	Yuasa B68-12V-36Ah
Electrical system	12V, 200W alternator, electronic current regulator	Secondary drive	1:2.533 (15/38) ⅝x⅜in Renold chain, 106 links
Battery	Yuasa 12N-12A-4A	Rear suspension	Twin Marzocchi 320mm shock absorbers, five-way adjustable for spring preload
Primary drive	Helical gear (32/70) 1:2.187	Rear tyre	120/90 H18 Metzeler C88, Pirelli

	MT18, 4.00x18 Metzeler C66
Rear tyre pressure	2.5-2.7kg/cm² (35.6-38.4 lb/sq.in)
Front brake	Dual Brembo P2F08N twin-piston calipers, Brembo master cylinder, 280mm discs
Length	2220mm
Max. height	1110mm
Max. width	735mm
Seat height	780mm

Colours 860 GTS and 900 GTS

Bodywork colour	Stripe colour
Pearl Orange	Black
Red/Orange	Silver
Black	Gold
Pearl Light Blue	Silver
Amaranth	Black
Green Scotland	Silver
Blue	Silver
Pearl Green	Silver

Specifications Ducati 750 and 900 SS 1977-78 (differing from 1975)

Motor denomination	DM 750.1 (750 SS), DM860.1 or DM 860 (900 SS)
Frame homologation	DM750SS or DM860SS
Homologation certificate	DGM 11871 OM (900 SS)
Racing camshaft	Valve timing (inlet) Inlet opens 65 degrees BTDC, closes 95 degrees ABDC ±5 degrees, 0.2mm
Racing camshaft	Valve timing (exhaust) Exhaust opens 95 degrees BBDC, closes 55 degrees ATDC ±5 degrees, 0.2mm
Ignition	Electronic, automatic advance 28 degrees at 2000rpm, total advance 34-36 degrees (750 SS), 32-34 degrees (900 SS) Bosch 6-32 degrees (1978)
Spark plugs	Champion UL82Y (0.8mm gap)
Carburettors	2 Dell'Orto PHF32AD/AS, 118/122 main jet, 60 pilot jet, 70/2 slide, K6 needle 2nd notch, 265AB needle jet, 75 start jet, 7450-1 float
Secondary drive	750 SS (Italian homologation) 1:2.125 (16/34)
	750 SS, 900 SS (Lafranconi, 32mm) 1:2.533 (15/38)
	900 SS (Italian homologation) 1:2.250 (16/36)

	(15/36)
Front Suspension	Marzocchi 38 mm telescopic fork (230cc ATF Dexron per leg)
Front tyre	Pirelli or Michelin 3.50V18,
Front tyre pressure	2.2-2.3kg/cm² (32 lb/sq.in)
Rear tyre	Pirelli 120/90V18 or Michelin 4.25/85V18,
Rear tyre pressure	2.3-2.7kg/cm² (33.43-37.69 lb/sq.in)
Fuel capacity (steel tank)	18-litres (2.5-litre reserve)

Specifications Ducati 900 Sport Desmo 'Darmah' 1977-78 (differing from 900 SS)

Motor denomination	DM860
Frame homologation	DM860SS
Homologation certificate	DGM 13715 OM
Compression ratio	9.3:1
Max. rpm	7, 800 rpm
Carburettors	2 Dell'Orto PHF32AD/AS, 122/118 main jet, 60 pilot jet, 70/2 slide, K6 needle 2nd notch, 265AB needle jet
Ignition	Electronic, automatic advance 6 degrees at 900rpm, 16 degrees at 1800rpm, 28 degrees at 2800rpm, 32 degrees at 4000rpm
Battery	Yuasa B68-12V-36Ah
Secondary drive	1:2.500 (16/40) ⅝x⅜in Renold chain, 108 links
Front Suspension	Ceriani or Marzocchi 38mm telescopic fork
Rear suspension	Twin 300mm (315mm) Marzocchi shock absorbers, five-way adjustable for spring preload
Front wheel	Campagnolo or Speedline 2.15x18in
Front tyre	Michelin 3.50H18
Front tyre pressure	2.2-2.3kg/cm² (31.3-32.7 lb/sq.in)
Rear wheel	Campagnolo or Speedline 2.50x18in
Rear tyre	Michelin 4.25/85V18
Rear tyre pressure	2.5-2.7kg/cm² (35.6-38.4 lb/sq.in)
Front brake	Brembo P2F08N twin piston caliper 280mm twin disc
Rear brake	Brembo P2F08N twin piston caliper 280mm disc
Front fork capacity	185cc AGIP OSO 25 in each leg
Oil sump capacity	5-litres Agip Sint 2000 SAE 10W50
Fuel tank capacity	15-litres
Wheelbase	1550mm
Length	2260mm
Max. height	1090mm
Max. width	780mm
Ground clearance	170mm
Seat height	780mm

Specifications Ducati 900 Sport Desmo 'Darmah' 1979-82 (differing from 1977-78)

Frame homologation	DM860SS or DM900SD
Homologation certificate	DGM 13715 OM or DGM 19139 OM
Spark plugs	Bosch W7B (W175T35) 0.6mm gap
Carburettors	2 Dell'Orto PHF32CD/CS, 122 main jet, 55 pilot jet, 60/3 slide, K16 needle 2nd notch, pump jet 38 (1979)
Secondary drive	1:2.533 (15/38) ⅝x⅜in Renold BS chain
Front suspension	Marzocchi 38mm telescopic fork
Rear suspension	Twin 330mm Marzocchi shock absorbers, five-way adjustable for spring preload
Front wheel	Speedline or FPS 2.15x18in
Front tyre	Pirelli 3.50H18
Rear wheel	Speedline or FPS 2.50x18in
Rear tyre	Pirelli 120/90 V18

Uprating kit for 900 SD and 900 SSD

On 25 January 1979 the factory released an official uprating kit for the Darmah and Darmah Super Sport that included:

Conti mufflers
Throttle cables
Dell'Orto PHM 40AD carburettors and manifolds
Dell'Orto PHM 40AS carburettors and manifolds
36-tooth rear sprocket

Modifications needed to be made to the rear carburettor bell mouth for the side cover to be fitted, and also the throttle cutaway so as to pull the 40mm throttles the full length of the throttle body.

Specifications Ducati 900 SS 1979-80 (differing from 1977-78)

Spark plugs	Bosch W7B (W175T35) 0.6mm gap
Carburettors	2 Dell'Orto PHF32CD/CS, 122 main jet, 55 pilot jet, 60/3 slide, K16 needle 2nd notch, pump jet 38
Front wheel	Speedline or FPS 2.15x18in
Front tyre	Michelin or Pirelli 100/90V18
Front tyre pressure	2 -2.3 kg/cm² (28.5-32.7 lb/sq.in)
Rear wheel	Speedline or FPS 2.50x18in
Rear tyre	Michelin or Pirelli 110/90V18
Rear tyre pressure	2.5-2.7 kg/cm² (35.6-38.4 lb/sq.in)
Rear brake	Brembo P2F08N twin piston caliper 280mm disc

Specifications Ducati 900 Super Sport Desmo 'Darmah' 1979-81 (differing from 900 SD)

Frame homologation	DM860SS or DM900SD
Homologation certificate	DGM 13715 OM or DGM 19139 OM
Compression ratio	9.5:1
Secondary drive	1:2.400 (15/36) ⅝x⅜in Renold BS chain
Front tyre	Pirelli 3.50H18
Rear tyre	Pirelli 120/90V18
Max. height	1280mm
Max. width	700mm

Specifications Ducati 900 MHR 1980 (differing from 900 SS)

Motor denomination	DM860
Frame homologation	DM860SS
Homologation certificate	DGM 13715 OM
Power	69 horsepower at 7000rpm with PHF 32 carbs
	80 horsepower at 7000rpm with PHM 40 carbs
Torque	8kgm at 5250rpm (PHF 32)
	8.8kgm at 5750rpm (PHM 40)
Max engine rpm	7500rpm
Carburettors	2 Dell'Orto PHF32CD/CS, 122 main jet, 55 pilot jet, 60/3 slide, K16 needle 2nd notch, pump jet 38
	2 Dell'Orto PHM40BD/ES, 135/140 main jet, 60 pilot jet, 60/1 slide, K5 2nd notch
Secondary drive	1:2.400 (15/36) ⅝x⅜in Regina Grand Prix 136 chain
Rear suspension	Twin Marzocchi 330mm shock absorbers, five-way adjustable for spring preload
Front wheel	Speedline or Campagnolo 2.15x18in
Front tyre	Pirelli Phantom 100/90V18
Front tyre pressure	2-2.3kg/cm² (28.5-32.7lb/sq.in)
Rear wheel	Speedline or Campagnolo 2.50x18in
Rear tyre	Pirelli Phantom 110/90V18
Rear tyre pressure	2.5-2.7kg/cm² (35.6-37.69lb/sq.in)
Rear brake	Brembo P2F08N twin piston caliper, 280mm disc
Fuel tank capacity	18-litres (24-litres second series)
Wheelbase	1510mm
Length	2200mm
Max. height	1280mm
Max. width	700mm
Seat height	800mm
Dry weight	205kg
Max speed	220km/h (with PHM 40 carbs)
Fuel consumption	5.8 l/100km
Range	300km

Specifications Ducati 900 Super Sport 1981-82 (differing from 1979-80)

Max engine rpm	7800
Compression ratio	9:3:1
Max power	57 horsepower at 7400rpm
Max torque	6.38kgm at 6000rpm
Secondary drive	1:2.375 (16/38)
Front fork capacity	280cc AGIP ATF Dexron in each leg
Front tyre	Michelin or Pirelli 3.50V18 100/90V18
Front tyre pressure	2.65kg/cm²
Rear tyre	Michelin or Pirelli 4.25/85V18, 110/90V18
Rear tyre pressure	2.9kg/cm²
Length	2210mm
Max. height	1220mm
Max. width	690mm
Seat height	840mm
Dry weight	205kg
Max speed	200km/h

Specifications Ducati 900 MHR 1981-83 (differing from 1980)

Motor denomination	DM860
Frame homologation	DM900R
Homologation certificate	DGM 50235 OM
Compression ratio	9:3:1
Power	63 horsepower at 7400rpm
Torque	7.02kgm at 5400
Max engine rpm	7900rpm
Carburettors	2 Dell'Orto PHM40BD/BS, 135/140 main jet, 60 pilot jet, 60/1 slide, K5 2nd notch
Secondary drive	1:2.200 (15/33)
Front tyre	Michelin or Pirelli 3.50V18, 100/90V18
Front tyre pressure	2.65kg/cm²
Rear tyre	Michelin or Pirelli 4.25/85V18, 110/90V18
Rear tyre pressure	2.9kg/cm²
Fuel tank capacity	24-litres
Wheelbase	1500mm
Length	2250mm
Max. height	1250mm
Dry weight	210.5kg
Max speed	222km/h

Specifications Ducati 900 S2 1983-84 (differing from 900 SS)

Frame homologation	DM900SS or DM900S2 (1984)
Homologation certificate	DGM 51148 OM (electric start)
Power	72 horsepower at 7500rpm

	32A for France)
Battery	Yuasa 12V-19Ah
Secondary drive	1:2.200 (15/33) Tsubaki 530 HSL 100 link chain
Front tyre	Pirelli 100/90V18
Rear tyre	Pirelli 110/90V18
Fuel tank capacity	18-litres
Width	690mm
Length	2220mm
Max. height	1250mm
Dry weight	190kg
Max speed	Over 205km/h

Specifications Ducati 900 MHR 1984 (differing from 1983)

Motor denomination	DM860
Frame homologation	DM900R1
Homologation certificate	DGM 51147 OM
Power	72 horsepower at 7000rpm
Torque	7.9kgm at 6000rpm
Max engine rpm	7800rpm
Clutch	Dry multiplate
Ignition	Bosch electronic, automatic advance 5 degrees/28 degrees
Battery	Yuasa 12V-19Ah
Front wheel	Oscam MT2.15x18in
Front tyre	Michelin A48 100/90V18
Front tyre pressure	2.33kg/cm²
Rear wheel	Oscam MT2.50x18in
Rear tyre	Michelin M48 120/90V18
Rear tyre pressure	2.6kg/cm²
Length	2220mm
Dry weight	212.5kg

Specifications Ducati 1000 MHR 1985-86 (differing from 900 MHR 1984)

Motor denomination	ZDM1000 or ZDM1000L
Frame homologation	ZDM1000R
Homologation certificate	DGM 51429 OM.
Bore	88mm
Stroke	80mm
Capacity	973cc
Power	76 horsepower at 6700rpm
Torque	8.6kgm at 5500rpm
Max engine rpm	7500rpm
Primary drive	Helical gear (39/69) 1:1.769
First	1:2.720 (17/37 x 24/30)
Second	1:1.761 (22/31 x 24/30)
Third	1:1.250 (27/27 x 24/30)
Fourth	1:1.000 direct drive
Fifth	1:0.887 (31/22 x 24/30)
Secondary drive	1:2.733 (15/41)
Rear tyre	Michelin M48 130/90V18
Dry weight	198kg

Specifications Ducati 1000 S2 1985 (differing from 1000 MHR)

Frame homologation	ZDM1000S2 or ZDM1000R

Production figures

860 GT and 860 (900) GTS	1974	1975	1976	1977	1978	1979	TOTAL
860 GT	568	477					1045
860 GT USA	776						776
860 electric start	244	250					494
860 electric start USA	83						83
860 GT electric start twin disc		351					351
860 GT electric start twin disc USA		238					238
860 GTS Europe		570	510	458	220	110	1868
860 GTS USA				242	30	40	312
	1671	1886	510	700	250	150	5167

750 Super Sport	1975	1976	1977	1978	TOTAL
750 Super Sport	249	120			369
750 Super Sport homologation		100	100	30	230
	249	220	100	30	599

900 Super Sport	1975	1976	1977	1978	1979	1980	1981	1982	TOTAL
900 SS (not homologation)	246	280							526
900 SS homologation Europe		520	496	924	774	713	1085	335	4847
900 SS homologation Germany				60					60
	246	1020	633	1017	934	753	1165	335	6103

900 SD	1977	1978	1979	1980	1981	1982	TOTAL
900 SD 'Darmah'	1610	1671	747	390	643	317	5378
900 SD 'Darmah' USA		20	80	80	40		220
	1610	1691	827	470	683	317	5598

900 SSD	1978	1979	1980	1981	TOTAL
900 SS 'Darmah'	200	309	345		854
900 SS 'Darmah' England			100		100
900 SS 'Darmah' USA		100			100
900 SS 'Darmah' Australia			260	126	386
	200	409	705	126	1440

MHR	1979	1980	1981	1982	1983	1984	198	1986	TOTAL
900 MHR kick	300	447	1500	1549	780	25			4601
900 MHR electric					687	770			1457
1000 MHR						662	199	250	1111
	300	447	1500	1549	1467	1457	199	250	7169

S2	1982	1983	1984	1985	TOTAL
900 S2 kick start	173	180			353
900 S2 electric start	476	202	205		883
1000 S2			71	100	171
	649	382	276	100	1407

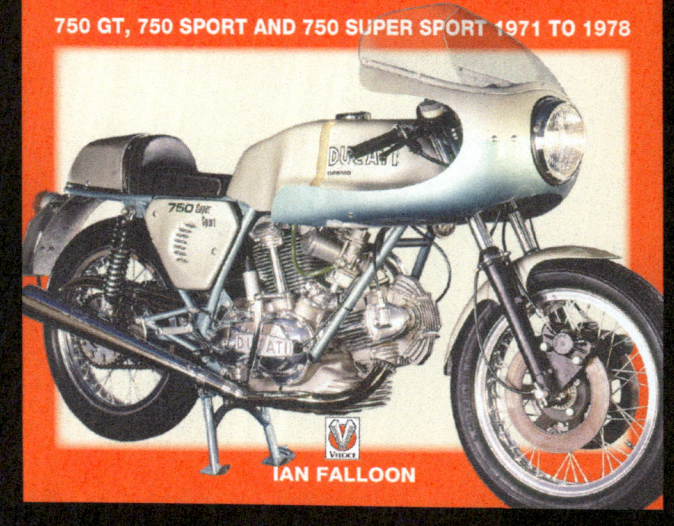

THE DUCATI 750 BIBLE

750 GT, 750 SPORT AND 750 SUPER SPORT 1971 TO 1978

IAN FALLOON

When the great Ducati engineer Fabio Taglioni designed the 750 Ducati in 1970 there was no way he could comprehend how important this model would be. The 750, the Formula 750 racer and the Super Sport became legend: this book celebrates these machines. Year-by-year, model-by-model, change-by-change detail.
Paperback • 25x20.7cm • 160 pages • 163 colour & b&w illustrations. ISBN: 978-1-787114-46-3

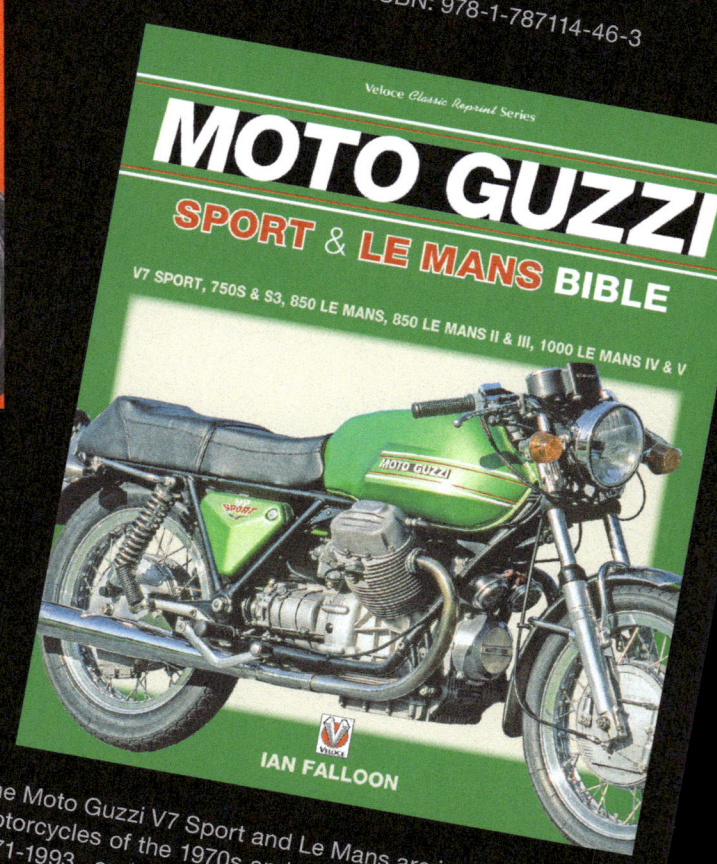

Veloce Classic Reprint Series

MOTO GUZZI
SPORT & LE MANS BIBLE

V7 SPORT, 750S & S3, 850 LE MANS, 850 LE MANS II & III, 1000 LE MANS IV & V

IAN FALLOON

The Moto Guzzi V7 Sport and Le Mans are iconic sporting motorcycles of the 1970s and 1980s. Covering the period 1971-1993, and all models with a description of model development year-by-year, full production data and 160 photos, this is a highly informative book and an essential Bible for enthusiasts.
Paperback • 25x20.7cm • 160 pages • 160 colour & b&w illustrations. ISBN: 978-1-787110-95-3

Veloce Classic Reprint Series

THE LAVERDA
TWINS & TRIPLES BIBLE
650 & 750cc Twins • 1000 & 1200cc Triples

IAN FALLOON

The large capacity Laverda twins and triples were some of the most charismatic and exciting motorcycles produced in a golden era. With a successful endurance racing program publicizing them, Laverda's twins soon earned a reputation for durability. Here is the year-by-year, model-by-model, change-by-change record.
Paperback • 25x20.7cm • 160 pages • 222 colour & b&w illustrations.
ISBN: 978-1-787110-48-9

The book of the

DUCATI 750 SS

'Round-case' 1974

Ian Falloon

Although manufactured for only one year, 1974, the Ducati 750 Super Sport was immediately touted as a future classic. It was a pioneer motorcycle – expensive and rare, and produced by Ducati's race department to celebrate victory in the 1972 Imola 200 Formula 750 race; for Ducatisti, it is the Holy Grail.

ISBN: 978-1-84584-202-4
Hardback • 25x25cm • 176 pages • 259 colour and b&w pictures

INDEX

Printed and bound by CPI Group (UK) Ltd, Croydon, CR0 4YY

21/04/2026

02094640-0004